Cincinnati Police Department Traffic Stops

Applying RAND's Framework to Analyze Racial Disparities

Greg Ridgeway

Sponsored by the City of Cincinnati

RAND
Center on Quality Policing
A RAND INFRASTRUCTURE, SAFETY, AND ENVIRONMENT CENTER

The research described in this report was sponsored by the City of Cincinnati and was conducted under the auspices of the RAND Center on Quality Policing within the Safety and Justice Program of RAND Infrastructure, Safety, and Environment (ISE).

Library of Congress Cataloging-in-Publication Data

Ridgeway, Greg, 1973–
Cincinnati Police Department traffic stops : applying RAND's framework to analyze racial disparities / Greg Ridgeway.
p. cm.
Includes bibliographical references.
ISBN 978-0-8330-4789-2 (pbk. : alk. paper)
1. Discrimination in law enforcement—Ohio—Cincinnati. 2. Racial profiling in law enforcement—Ohio—Cincinnati. 3. Police—Ohio—Cincinnati—Attitudes. 4. Traffic violations—Ohio—Cincinnati. 5. Race discrimination—Ohio—Cincinnati. 6. Cincinnati (Ohio). Police Dept. I. Title.

HV8148.C52R53 2009
363.2'32—dc22

2009032441

Published 2009 by the RAND Corporation
1776 Main Street, P.O. Box 2138, Santa Monica, CA 90407-2138
1200 South Hayes Street, Arlington, VA 22202-5050
4570 Fifth Avenue, Suite 600, Pittsburgh, PA 15213-2665
RAND URL: http://www.rand.org/
To order RAND documents or to obtain additional information, contact
Distribution Services: Telephone: (310) 451-7002;
Fax: (310) 451-6915; Email: order@rand.org

Preface

This is the fifth and final annual report that the RAND Corporation has produced on police-community relations in Cincinnati, Ohio. The reports are required under RAND's contract to evaluate whether an agreement on police-community relations in Cincinnati is achieving its goals. The collaborative agreement was reached in 2002, when the Cincinnati Police Department (CPD) joined with other agencies and organizations (collectively referred to here as *the parties*) to enact a series of reforms and initiatives intended to improve police-community relations in the city. This final report focuses exclusively on the analysis of racial disparities in traffic stops in Cincinnati.

This monograph should be of interest to policymakers and community members in Cincinnati and may also prove useful to residents and officials in other jurisdictions that are confronting similar issues. The City of Cincinnati funded this project on behalf of the parties to the collaborative agreement. Reports from earlier years (Riley et al., 2005; Ridgeway, Schell, Riley, et al., 2006; Schell et al., 2007; Ridgeway, Schell, Gifford, et al., 2009) are freely available from RAND. Other recent and related RAND works that may be of interest to readers of this report include the following:

- *Analysis of Racial Disparities in the New York Police Department's Stop, Question, and Frisk Practices* (Ridgeway, 2007)
- *Evaluation of the New York City Police Department Firearm Training and Firearm-Discharge Review Process* (Rostker et al., 2008)
- "Assessing the Effect of Race Bias in Post–Traffic Stop Outcomes Using Propensity Scores" (Ridgeway, 2006)

- "Testing for Racial Profiling in Traffic Stops from Behind a Veil of Darkness" (Grogger and Ridgeway, 2006)
- "Doubly Robust Internal Benchmarking and False Discovery Rates for Detecting Racial Bias in Police Stops" (Ridgeway and MacDonald, 2009).

The RAND Center on Quality Policing

This research was conducted under the auspices of the RAND Center on Quality Policing within the Safety and Justice Program of RAND Infrastructure, Safety, and Environment (ISE). The center conducts research and analysis to improve contemporary police practice and policy. The mission of ISE is to improve the development, operation, use, and protection of society's essential physical assets and natural resources and to enhance the related social assets of safety and security of individuals in transit and in their workplaces and communities. Safety and Justice Program research addresses occupational safety, transportation safety, food safety, and public safety—including violence, policing, corrections, substance abuse, and public integrity.

Questions or comments about this monograph should be sent to the project leader, Greg Ridgeway (Greg_Ridgeway@rand.org). Information about the Safety and Justice Program is available online (http://www.rand.org/ise/safety), as is information about the Center on Quality Policing (http://cqp.rand.org). Inquiries about research projects should be sent to the following address:

Greg Ridgeway, Director
Safety and Justice Program, ISE
RAND Corporation
1776 Main Street
Santa Monica, CA 90407-2138
310-393-0411 x7734
Greg_Ridgeway@rand.org

Contents

Figures

Tables

Summary

Introduction

In Cincinnati, a memorandum of agreement (MOA) between the city and the U.S. Department of Justice (DOJ), dated April 12, 2002, sought to remedy a pattern or practice of conduct by law-enforcement officers that deprives individuals of rights, privileges, or immunities secured by the U.S. Constitution or federal law. Separately in 2002, the City of Cincinnati and other parties (collectively, *the parties*) entered into a collaborative agreement in an attempt to resolve social conflict, improve community-police relations, reduce crime and disorder, and resolve pending individual and organizational legal claims about racially biased policing in Cincinnati. In July 2004, the city, on behalf of the parties of the collaborative agreement, hired the RAND Corporation to conduct evaluations over the course of five years to assist the parties with measuring progress toward the goals of the collaborative agreement.

This monograph represents the final annual report, for the fifth year. While the evaluations in the previous years covered a large series of tasks, this evaluation focuses solely on three assessments of the traffic-stop data: (1) an assessment of whether there is a department-wide pattern of bias against black drivers in the decision to stop a vehicle, (2) an assessment of the fraction of CPD officers who disproportionately stop black drivers compared to other officers patrolling the same neighborhoods at the same time, and (3) an assessment of racial biases in post-stop outcomes, including stop duration, citation rates, and search rates.

Findings

In assessing *whether there is a department-wide pattern of bias against black drivers in the decision to stop a vehicle*, we take an approach that is different from the traditional approaches to creating an external benchmark—all of which have some limitations; our approach gets around those limitations by taking advantage of a natural experiment involving daylight saving time (DST) that does not require explicit external estimates of the racial or ethnic distribution of those at risk of being stopped. More specifically, to assess bias in the decision to stop, we compare stops immediately before and immediately after changes to and from DST, when a similar mix of drivers and a similar allocation of police officers will be in effect and in which the only major difference will be in officers' ability to see, because of the shift from daylight to darkness, the race of the drivers being stopped.

From that assessment, we found the following, for 2008:

- Black drivers were less likely to be stopped during daylight, when drivers' races are more visible, evidence that is counter to what we would expect if there were racial profiling.
- Aggregating six years of data, from 2003 to 2008, we find no evidence of racial profiling in officers' decisions to stop drivers.

In assessing *whether there is racial bias in the decision to stop at the individual officer level*, we use an internal-benchmarking approach that constructs a customized internal benchmark for each officer, comparing the racial distribution of suspects stopped by the officer in question with the racial distribution of suspects stopped by other officers at the same times and places and in the same contexts. This method selects an officer, identifies stops that other officers made at the same time and in the same neighborhood, and compares the racial distributions of the stopped drivers. Since the officers are patrolling the same areas at the same times, the racial distributions should be the same (assuming that the officers are on the same assignment).

When we conduct the internal-benchmarking assessment, we find the following:

- Ten officers appear to be stopping significantly more black drivers than did other officers patrolling at the same times and places and in the same contexts.

In assessing *whether there is racial bias or disparities in what happens after the stop*—in the length of the stop, in the rates at which officers cite motorists, and in the way they conduct vehicle searches—we use a method known as propensity-score weighting to identify stops involving nonblack drivers that are similarly situated to the stops involving black drivers and make post-stop comparisons between the two groups. Doing so allows us to account for a large number of factors—such as neighborhood, place of residence, reason for stop, day and month of stop, time of day of stop, state of vehicle registration, validity of the driver's license, and number and age of occupants in vehicle—that can confound whether the differences we see in post-stop outcomes are actually the result of racial bias.

When we conduct the propensity-score weighting analysis of post-stop decisions, we find the following:

- Black drivers who were stopped were slightly more likely to have their stops exceed 10 minutes, compared to similarly situated nonblack drivers who were stopped.
- There was no racial difference in the percentage of stops lasting more than 30 minutes when comparing black drivers to similarly situated nonblack drivers.
- Black drivers were less likely to receive a citation than were similarly situated nonblack drivers.
- Officers were less likely to conduct a high-discretion search, such as a consent search, of a black driver than of a similarly situated nonblack driver.
- When searched, black and nonblack drivers were equally likely to be found in possession of contraband.

If we do not limit the compared drivers to those in similar situations, we do find large differences. For example, officers more frequently search black drivers than nonblack drivers (13 percent versus

6 percent). While this disparity is largely due to differences in when, where, and why the stops occurred, these differences in experience can shape black drivers' views of CPD officers.

Conclusions and Implications

Although we found no evidence of racial differences between the stops of black and those of similarly situated nonblack drivers, there are issues that can exacerbate the perception of racial bias. First, for each year of analysis, we find several officers who stop substantially more black drivers than their peers do. These represent a small fraction of CPD officers, and, as noted in the document, CPD has the capability to monitor, manage, and address issues that these officers may present to the department and the community. Second, although black and similarly situated nonblack drivers have similar stop outcomes, the burden of policing falls disproportionately on black residents, even though nonblack drivers have similar stop outcomes.

There are still substantial gaps between how black and nonblack residents view CPD. As noted in last year's RAND report (Ridgeway, Schell, Gifford, et al., 2009), the improvements that have been seen over the life of the collaborative agreement may be fragile. It will require a continued and concerted effort on the part of CPD and community leaders to maintain progress toward the goals stated in the collaborative agreement, as well as to prevent reversals in the positive trends that we observed while this agreement was in force.

Acknowledgments

I gratefully acknowledge the comments of two independent reviewers and the parties to the collaborative agreement. In the years of this study, John Eck, professor in the Division of Criminal Justice at the University of Cincinnati and a nationally recognized expert on policing, has consistently helped sharpen the focus and presentation. We benefited immensely from his knowledge of policing and his great familiarity with Cincinnati. Lois Davis, a senior policy researcher and my colleague at RAND, helped clarify several sections of this monograph.

Paul Steinberg carefully polished this monograph so that it would not merely report statistics on the 2008 traffic stops but also describe RAND's approach to racial-profiling analysis, providing a road map for Cincinnati and other cities asking similar questions.

Lisa Bernard has edited and formatted nearly 1,000 pages of RAND reports on police-community relations in Cincinnati, and I greatly appreciate her attention to detail and her timeliness.

The staff of the Cincinnati Police Department has been of great assistance, responding promptly to data requests and clarifying policies. Lt. Col. Cindy Combs, Lt. Daniel R. Ogilvie, Lt. Debbie Bauer, Gerald L. Geisel, and Vanessa Smedley were instrumental in this effort.

Although I have benefited from others, I alone remain responsible for errors and omissions in this analysis.

Abbreviations

CAD	computer-aided dispatch
CBD	Central Business District
CPD	Cincinnati Police Department
CPOP	Community Problem-Oriented Policing
DOJ	U.S. Department of Justice
DST	daylight saving time
fdr	false-discovery rate
IRB	institutional review board
ISE	RAND Infrastructure, Safety, and Environment
LAPD	Los Angeles Police Department
MOA	memorandum of agreement
TEAMS	Training Evaluation and Management System

CHAPTER ONE

Introduction

Background

Many police departments nationwide, including the Cincinnati Police Department (CPD), face expensive civil litigation because of high-profile police use-of-force incidents and allegations of patterns of racially biased police practices.

In Cincinnati, a memorandum of agreement (MOA) between the city and the U.S. Department of Justice (DOJ), dated April 12, 2002, sought to remedy a pattern or practice of conduct by law-enforcement officers that deprives individuals of rights, privileges, or immunities secured by the U.S. Constitution or federal law (U.S. Department of Justice, City of Cincinnati, Ohio, and Cincinnati Police Department, 2002, paragraph II.1). This agreement followed a 2001 DOJ review of CPD use of force. Subsequent to the review, the DOJ recommended changes in CPD's policies and procedures and the city's internal mechanism for resolving citizen complaints. The DOJ and the city concluded that the MOA, rather than litigation, was the appropriate way to resolve the city remediation of the DOJ's findings.

Separately in 2002, the City of Cincinnati and other parties (collectively, *the parties*) entered into a collaborative agreement in an attempt to resolve social conflict, improve community-police relations, reduce crime and disorder, and resolve pending individual and organizational legal claims about racially biased policing in Cincinnati. The goals spelled out in the collaborative agreement were as follows:

- [Ensure that p]olice officers and community members . . . become proactive partners in community problem solving.
- Build relationships of respect, cooperation, and trust within and between police and communities.
- Improve education, oversight, monitoring, hiring practices, and accountability of . . . CPD.
- Ensure fair, equitable, and courteous treatment for all.
- Create methods to establish the public's understanding of police policies and procedures and recognition of exceptional service in an effort to foster support for the police (*In re Cincinnati Policing*, 2003, pp. 3–4).

As noted in the collaborative agreement itself, "this Agreement is outcome oriented, putting great emphasis on objective measures of police-citizen relations and police effectiveness" (*In re Cincinnati Policing*, 2003, p. 4). Accordingly, the parties agreed to establish an evaluation process that would support their mutual accountability plan.

In July 2004, the city, on behalf of the parties, hired the RAND Corporation to conduct evaluations over the course of five years to assist the parties with measuring progress toward the goals of the collaborative agreement.[1] The individual elements of the evaluation, referred to as *tasks*, have been combined into annual reports.

Objectives and Scope

This monograph represents the final annual report, for the fifth year. Over the five years, the RAND evaluations have covered a series of tasks:

- The community-police satisfaction survey tracked community perceptions about CPD by seeking to determine the degree to which Cincinnati residents trust and are satisfied with CPD.

[1] The RAND evaluation has addressed the provisions of the collaborative agreement, not the provisions of the MOA with the DOJ; however, the MOA's provisions serve as an important backdrop to the collaborative agreement.

- A traffic-stop analysis analyzed traffic-stop patterns to investigate whether racial biases influence police activities in the decision to stop, cite, and search vehicles in Cincinnati.
- Analysis of audio and video recordings from cameras mounted in CPD patrol cars shed light on the origins of police-community conflict and dissatisfaction.
- Analysis of CPD staffing examined CPD statistics on recruitment, retention, and promotion for their implications for officer morale and job satisfaction.
- Assessment of problem-solving processes observed in community council and Community Problem-Oriented Policing (CPOP) meetings to provide important insights into CPD's implementation, and the community's acceptance and utilization, of the CPOP process.
- The police-citizen interaction survey asked citizens who interacted with police to describe the reason for their interaction, their perceptions of police conduct and professionalism, their recollections of the officer's knowledge about the citizen's problem, the clarity of officer's instructions for seeking help or resolving the problem, and basic demographic information about the citizen.
- Surveys of the complaint process and internal review asked participants in the official complaint process to assess the perceived fairness of the complaint process, the level of input that both citizens and officers have into the process, and outcome of the process and to give their thoughts on how to improve the process.
- The police-officer survey asked CPD officers whose duties entail significant interaction with citizens for their perceptions of personal safety, citizen support, working conditions, officer morale, organizational barriers to effective policing, and perceptions of fairness in evaluation and promotion.

As specified in the contract, every task was not completed in each of the five years. Table 1.1 shows the years in which the specific tasks were scheduled. As shown, three tasks were completed in report year 1 and not repeated, one task was completed in report years 1 and 4, and two tasks were completed in report years 1, 2, and 4. As shown by the

Table 1.1
Schedule of Reports and Contents

	Report Year				
Task	**1**	**2**	**3**	**4**	**5**
Incident year covered by CPD data[a]	2003–2004[b]	2005	2006	2007	2008
Statistical compilations	Yes	Yes	Yes	Yes	No
Community satisfaction survey	Yes	No	No	Yes	No
Traffic-stop data analysis	Yes	Yes	Yes	Yes	Yes
Audio and video analysis	Yes	Yes	Yes	Yes	No
CPD staffing	Yes	No	No	No	No
Problem-solving process	Yes	No	No	No	No
Police-citizen interaction survey	Yes	No	No	No	No
Complaint process	Yes	Yes	No	Yes	No
Officer survey	Yes	Yes	No	Yes	No

[a] CPD provides data on statistical compilations, staffing, and motor-vehicle stops, as well as tapes of motor-vehicle stops. RAND collected all other data directly in the year in which the report was written.

[b] Both 2003 and 2004 data were used for the motor vehicle–stop task only in the year 1 evaluation.

shading, one task—the traffic-stop data analysis—was completed each year and is the sole subject of this fifth-year report.

The traffic-stop data-analysis task is divided into three assessments: (1) an assessment of whether there is a department-wide pattern of bias against black drivers in the decision to stop a vehicle, (2) an assessment of the fraction of CPD officers who disproportionately stop black drivers compared to other officers patrolling the same neighborhoods at the same time, and (3) an assessment of racial biases in post-stop outcomes, including stop duration, citation rates, and search rates.

Approach and Data

Each of the three assessments has its own methodology, which is discussed in detail in the three results sections that follow. In general, however, each assessment seeks to remove the effect of other plausible explanations for differences. This includes adjustments for when, where, and why stops occur. The aim is to isolate race's effect from that of other factors on the decision to stop, cite, and search vehicles.

In previous years, we developed statistical compilations of CPD data, as shown in the first row of Table 1.1. The statistical compilations addressed a range of topics, including arrests and reported crimes by neighborhood; vehicle stops and citation, search, and arrest rates by neighborhood; use-of-force incidents by neighborhood; and calls for service by neighborhood. RAND has reviewed the compilations each year to help establish the context of policing in Cincinnati, including how CPD allocates resources, the demand for police services, and how these factors vary relative to the racial composition of Cincinnati's neighborhoods.

In this way, the statistical compilations provide important inputs into other tasks of the contract. For example, analysis in RAND's earlier reports described how crime tends to be clustered in specific parts of the city at certain times of the day and week. In turn, this means that law-enforcement presence is going to be clustered in space and time in a way that correlates with the crime patterns. Most pertinent here, the traffic-stop analyses must take these clustering patterns into account, since the risk of exposure to law enforcement is not uniform in time and space.

Looking in more detail at the data underlying the three assessments, CPD's investigatory-stop policy requires officers to complete form 534, a citizen-contact card, for all motor-vehicle stops. Also, for any passenger detained separately, the officer must complete a separate form 534. The contact cards include information on the vehicle (license plate, car make, and year), the driver (race, age, and driver's license), passengers, and the stop (stop location, stop reason, whether a search occurred, stop outcome, and stop duration).[2] Our assessments rely primarily on the data from a database that CPD created from these contact cards for the 2008 calendar year.

CPD records the policing block in which the stop occurred and implements rigorous checks on address validity. Policing-block numbers correspond to one of 504 small geographic areas of the city. For any stop that occurred on a highway (interstates 275, 471, 71, 74, and 75, SR-126 [Ronald Reagan Cross County Highway], SR-562 [Norwood Lateral], the Red Bank Expressway, and the Sixth Street Expressway), we coded them as unique locations, replacing their policing-block labels with highway identifiers. About 1,000 stops (less 2 percent) in the database did not include valid policing blocks; however, by merging with computer-aided dispatch (CAD) logs and geocoding the addresses, we were able to resolve 100 percent of the stop locations.

We received data on 62,678 stops in 2008 (56,609 stops for motor-vehicle violations). For closer inspection of the completion rates, we obtained CAD logs from CPD. These CAD logs indicate the date and time of stop initiation, the stop's completion time, the stop location (address, policing block, and district), disposition, and an incident number. In 2008, CPD recorded 57,613 traffic stops in CAD that should have resulted in a contact card. For every traffic stop, CPD officers radio dispatch, indicating that they are involved in a traffic stop and unavailable to be redeployed elsewhere. All traffic stops that CPD officers conducted appear in CAD logs and should have an associated contact card (form 534) giving additional stop details. We used the CAD-log data to check whether the number of stops in the CAD logs matched the volume of contact cards.

In 2008, there were 1.7 percent more traffic stops recorded in CAD logs than in contact cards. This translates into 1,004 traffic stops that apparently occurred but were not documented with a contact card.

---

[2] CPD officers also completed contact cards for some pedestrian stops, collecting information on the individual detained and on stop attributes.

This gap is a smaller one than in previous years. Dispatchers can, at times, code as traffic stops certain investigations that should not generate a contact card, such as investigations of parked vehicles. This could account for these 1,004 undocumented apparent traffic stops.

Items from the contact cards were missing at times. In 2008, 0.3 percent of stops were missing at least one of the following: stop location, date, or time or driver age, race, or sex. This is essentially unchanged from 2006. Table 1.2 gives some more specific information on the types of fields that are important for our analyses and includes a comparison with prior years. The bottom line is that the quality of the traffic-stop data has greatly improved over the course of the study period. As shown in the shaded column, when compared to the comparable columns for 2004 through 2007 (from right to left), critical stop features, such as driver's race and stop location, were rarely missing; for the former, it was missing less than 0.3 percent of the time in 2008, compared to 6 percent in 2004.

Table 1.2
Missing Basic Stop Information from Motor-Vehicle Violations

Stop Feature	Missing Information (2008)		Missing Information (%)			
	n	%	2007	2006	2005	2004
Date	0	0.0	0.0	0.0		
Time	0	0.0	0.0	0.2	0.2	0.6
Duration	104	0.2	0.4	23.8	20.0	7.5
Location	0	0.0	0.0	0.1	0.7	1.7
Officer	0	0.0	0.0	0.0	0.6	1.6
Driver race	149	0.3	0.3	0.0	0.7	6.0
Driver sex	9	0.0	0.0	0.0	0.9	6.1
Driver age	2	0.0	0.1	0.0	1.7	6.9

NOTE: n is out of 56,609 stops for motor-vehicle violations.

Organization of This Monograph

The remainder of this monograph is organized around the three assessments that form the core of the traffic-stop analyses, providing results for the fifth year in the context of results from the preceding years. Chapter Two examines whether there is evidence of a department-wide pattern of targeting black drivers. Chapter Three assesses whether there are individual officers who seem to stop a disproportionate number of black drivers relative to their fellow officers patrolling in a similar context. Chapter Four examines the racial disparities in stop outcomes: stop duration, citation rates, search rates, and hit rates. Chapter Five draws the main conclusions from the research.

Appendix A contains more detail on the propensity-scoring approach that underlies much of the analysis here, while Appendix B discusses the approach used to estimate false-discovery rates. Appendix C contains details for analysis results that are summarized in the main document.

CHAPTER TWO

Is There a Department-Level Racial Pattern in Initiating Vehicle Stops?

Introduction

There is considerable concern about police racial profiling: Some 69 percent of black Americans say that the police treat them less fairly than whites (Ludwig, 2003), 53 percent of the American public believe that the practice of racial profiling is widespread, and 67 percent say that the practice is never justified (Gallup and Newport, 2006). This public concern about racial profiling has led to massive data-collection efforts to validate or invalidate whether the practice is taking place or, if it *is* taking place, to what extent.

Unfortunately, despite all the data collection that has occurred, there is still considerable confusion about how the data should be used to test for racial profiling. Many researchers in the field argue that a difference between the racial distribution of the persons stopped by the police and the racial distribution of the population at risk of being stopped constitutes *proof* that racial profiling exists (San Jose Police Department, 2002; Kadane and Terrin, 1997; Smith and Alpert, 2002; Mac Donald, 2001; Dominitz, 2003; GAO, 2000; Zingraff et al., 2000). However, in practice, the racial composition of the community is still often used as a proxy measure of the population at risk of being stopped.

By this latter argument, one might be led to conclude that there is racial profiling in Cincinnati. Census data from 2007 report that 44 percent of Cincinnati's residents are black (U.S. Census Bureau, 2007). In 2008, 53 percent of the stops involved black drivers, and, of those stops involving a Cincinnati resident (as opposed to drivers living outside Cincinnati), 63 percent involved a black driver. But these differences say little, if anything, about unequal treatment. For example, in the same data set, 66 percent of the drivers stopped were male, although the residential rate of males in Cincinnati is 47 percent; we believe that much of the difference, in this case, results from the fact that men might drive in the city more often and might be more likely to break traffic laws when they drive than women do, rather than the fact that officers are specifically targeting men—although this, too, is certainly possible.

We must reason in the same fashion when dealing with race rather than sex. In other words, we must ask whether something besides racial profiling can explain the difference between the observed rate at which black drivers are stopped and the stop rate expected if there were no bias. More specifically, to assess racial biases, analysis must be able to separate out (i.e., account for) three factors when comparing the racial distribution of stops:

1. *Differential rates of offending: Driving behavior might vary by race.* That is, black drivers may be stopped more often because they may be more likely to commit some kind of traffic infraction. This may include expired license plates, speeding, or mechanical violations. Some studies have shown differences by race in speeding (Lange, Blackman, and Johnson, 2002) and seatbelt use (Hallmark, Mueller, and Veneziano, 2004), but we do not know whether this is the case in Cincinnati.
2. *Differential rates of exposure: Exposure to law enforcement might vary by race.* Black drivers may be stopped more often because they are more likely to be exposed to law enforcement. They may drive more often, or, more likely, they may drive in regions with greater police presence; thus, any infraction they make would be more likely to be noticed, resulting in more stops.
3. *Differential rates of stopping by race: Police might be practicing racially biased policing.* Black drivers may be stopped more often because officers are actively seeking black drivers to stop. For example, when officers observe vehicles involved in some traffic

infraction, they might be more likely to stop the vehicle if the driver is black.

The difficulty in assessing a racial bias in traffic stops—the third factor—is in developing a reasonable expected rate, often known as the *benchmarking problem*. Any method that aims to assess a racial bias in the decision to stop a vehicle must be able to account for or rule out differences resulting from the first two factors for stops so that what remains is truly the result of the third factor. As a result, researchers have used different benchmarks to try to do this. One such external benchmark—the one discussed earlier—involves *comparisons to the residential census*, but such comparisons are inadequate, because they do not account for either of the first two factors for stops. Further confounding the comparisons is that a large fraction of motorists do not live in the neighborhoods in which police stopped them. In 2008, 22 percent of the drivers stopped in Cincinnati were not Cincinnati residents.

Several proposed benchmarking methods aim to assess the racial distribution of drivers on the streets either by posting observers on street corners or by using surrogate measures, such as the racial distribution of not-at-fault car crashes. While these methods might adjust for differential police exposure (factor 1), they do not adjust for different rates of offending (factor 2). Instead, such methods require the assumption that drivers from each racial group have equal rates of offenses, which may or may not be true. Studies have shown that almost all drivers have some vehicle-code violation while driving (Lamberth, 2003); however, police do not stop vehicles for all violations and are expected to use discretion when selecting certain offenses and certain vehicles for a traffic stop. We aim to assess whether this discretion differentially affects black drivers.

In the assessment described here, we take a different approach, one that gets around the benchmarking problem by taking advantage of a natural experiment involving daylight saving time (DST) that does not require explicit external estimates of the racial distribution of those at risk of being stopped. Using that assessment, we found that, *in 2008, black drivers were less likely to be stopped during daylight, when drivers' races are more visible, evidence that is counter to what we would expect if there were racial profiling. Aggregating six years of data, from 2003 to 2008, we find no evidence of racial profiling in officers' decisions to stop drivers.* The remainder of this chapter explains the approach we used and shows how this finding was derived.

What We Did

To assess racial bias in the decision to stop, we use a benchmarking method to which we refer as the *veil-of-darkness method*, described in Grogger and Ridgeway (2006). Fridell (2004, p. 123) also discusses this method, describing it as one for "benchmarking with data from 'blind' enforcement mechanisms."

In its basic form, our analysis compares the racial distribution of stops made during daylight to the racial distribution of stops made at night. If there were a practice of targeting black drivers, the effects of this profiling would be most pronounced during daylight, when the driver's race is most visible to the officer. While the race of some nighttime drivers might be visible, the rate of police knowing driver race in advance of the stop must be smaller at night than during daylight. In fact, there is evidence of this. Lamberth (2003) described a traffic survey in which the driver's race could be identified in 95 percent of the vehicles but for which nighttime observations required auxiliary lighting. Greenwald (2001) canceled plans for evening surveys after his observer could identify the race of only 6 percent of the drivers viewed around dusk.

An overly simplistic implementation of this analysis would compare the percentage of black drivers among those stopped during daylight with the percentage of black drivers among those stopped at night. However, things might be different during daylight from how they are at night. For example, even if there were no racially biased practices, we still may observe differences in the prevalence of black drivers among those stopped, daytime versus nighttime, if the mix of black and nonblack drivers on the road changes over the course of the day. And, in fact, differences in work schedules can cause changes in the mix of black and white drivers (Hamermesh, 1996).

Thus, to assess bias in the decision to stop, we took advantage of a natural experiment, DST, comparing stops immediately before and immediately after changes to and from DST. Every spring and fall, Cincinnati switches between Eastern DST and Eastern standard time. Put simply, on one Monday, it is light at 6:30 p.m., while, on the following Monday (one week later, after DST goes into effect), it is dark at 6:30 p.m. During both of these periods (in the spring and fall), we hypothesize that the mix of black and nonblack drivers on the road would not drastically change, the kinds of drivers who commit offenses for which police make stops would not change, and the patterns of police allocation would not change. The major difference between these two periods is the officers' ability to identify race in advance of the stop. As a result, such a comparison does not require explicit information on the characteristics of drivers at risk of being stopped.

In this way, we can separate out the differential rates of offending and exposure to police (factors 1 and 2) and concentrate on whether we see racial bias in stops (factor 3). Drivers at 7:00 p.m. are exposed to the same distribution of police on either side of the DST switch. While incidents will, from time to time, draw police to particular locations, according to CPD, the allocation of police effort does not suddenly change following the time change. As a result, this method is not as prone to errors from differential police exposure. The drivers who are likely to offend during daylight are also likely to be the ones who offend at nighttime. At night, the overall rate of offending might decrease (e.g., speeding in poorly lit areas might decrease). However, we assume that there is not a differential change in *relative* offending rates by race as daylight moves into nighttime.

In practice, for such an analysis, we use several weeks of data on either side of the transitions to and from DST. Table 2.1 shows the data in 2008, highlighting the data used for the veil-of-darkness analyses in the shaded rows. We conducted two analyses using the data. In the first analysis, we use only the 598 stops that represent all motor-violation

Table 2.1
Stops Used in the Veil-of-Darkness Analysis

Characteristic	Stops
Stops in data set	62,678
Motor-vehicle stop	56,609
Moving violations only	34,248
Race not missing	34,099
Evening stops (intertwilight period)	5,036
Evening spring stops (±30 days of DST)	304
Evening fall stops (±30 days of DST)	294

motor-vehicle stops[1] for which race is not missing[2] that occur 30 days before or after DST in the spring or fall within the *intertwilight period* (or a total of 120 days of stops out of 365 days of stops), shown in the bottom two rows of the table.

The intertwilight period is between 5:50 p.m. and about 8:06 p.m. During this period, stops may occur in either daylight or darkness, depending on the season. Stops before this time window always occur in daylight; after this time window, they are always in darkness. We isolated this group of stops because we believe that the racial mix of drivers on the road is more homogeneous during this limited period than during the rest of the year. There were relatively few reported stops in the morning hours, so we focused exclusively on evening stops. The estimates adjust for clock time to control for the possibility that the racial mix of drivers exposed to the police may change at different clock times.

---

1 We believe that headlight violations are a special case, in that they are noticed only at nighttime. Therefore, we removed all equipment violations from the analysis so that the method is not prone to such confounding. This accounts for the difference in Table 2.1 between total motor-vehicle stops (56,609) and motor violations only (34,248).

2 Recall from Table 1.2 in Chapter One that race is missing in 149 cases from the stop data. That accounts for the difference between 34,248 and 34,099 in Table 2.1.

The second analysis makes use of *all* stops in the intertwilight period (or a total of 365 days of stops, 5,036 stops in 2008, as shown in the third shaded row in the table). In this analysis, the racial mix of drivers on the road is less homogeneous because we are using all months and all seasons and, thus, from an analytic point of view, less useful; however, the analysis does make use of far more stops.

Clearly, the first analysis in particular (and the second analysis as well) excludes a large percentage of the available 34,099 recorded stops that could be used. However, the analyses focus on those stops that have the greatest potential to isolate the effect of racial bias.

We illustrate the experiment in the first analysis graphically in Figure 2.1. On the horizontal axis, we cover clock time during the intertwilight period—the period between 5:50 p.m. and about 8:06 p.m. The dots represent the 598 stops of black (filled dots) and white (unfilled dots) drivers over the 120 calendar days—30 days before and after DST in the fall and spring. The vertical axis shows

Figure 2.1
Stops of Black and Nonblack Drivers, by Darkness and Clock Time, Fall and Spring 2008

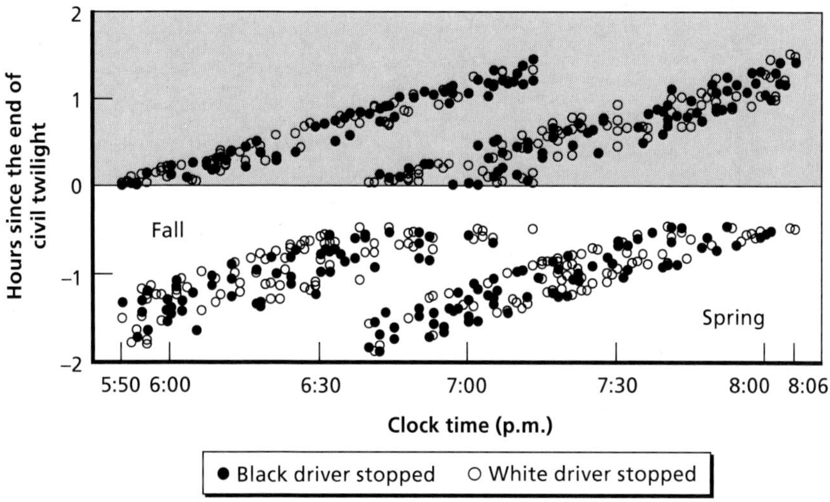

Calendar time covered: 120 days (30+ days before and after DST in fall and spring)
Total stops shown: 598
RAND *MG914-2.1*

the hours since the end of civil twilight, with the shaded area representing stops that occur when it is dark and the unshaded area representing those that occur when it is light. The intertwilight period is shifted to later in the day in spring, because of differences between spring and fall in the scheduling of DST changes, which explains the upward movement in the stops over clock time across the horizontal axis.

What We Found

Figure 2.2, which builds off Figure 2.1, illustrates the process we use in determining whether we see racial bias in the decision to stop drivers. Specifically, we show short time slices, in which we can compare the prevalence of black drivers among all stopped drivers, daylight

Figure 2.2
Percentage of Black Drivers Stopped, by Darkness and Clock Time, Fall and Spring 2008

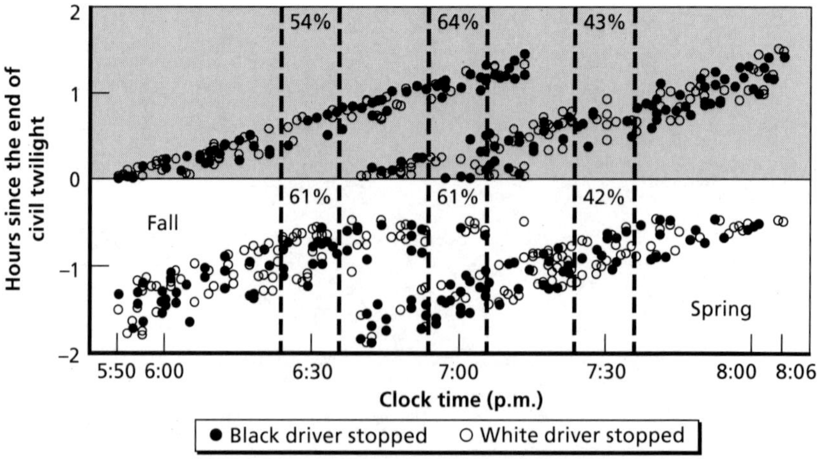

Calendar time covered: 120 days (30+ days before and after DST in fall and spring)
Total stops shown: 598

NOTE: Numbers within the bands indicate the percentage of drivers stopped in that time period who were black.

RAND *MG914-2.2*

versus darkness. Within these intervals, we computed the percentage of stopped drivers who were black. At 7:00 p.m., for example, 64 percent of the drivers stopped in darkness were black, and 61 percent of the drivers stopped in daylight were black. These statistics imply that, for these stops, officers essentially stop the same fraction of black drivers, regardless of whether a driver's race is visible. Note that all these stops occurred at 7:00 p.m., so the only likely difference between the daylight and darkness groups of drivers is visibility of race. Of course, there are too few stops at 7:00 p.m. to be conclusive. At 6:30, the data show that police stopped a greater percentage of black drivers during daylight, whereas, at 7:30, the stop percentages were about the same in darkness and daylight.

For the actual analysis, we average over all 598 stops across all time points, using logistic regression to estimate the race effect.[3] Averaging over all time points combines all the observations while still adjusting for clock time. In addition, we adjust for day of the week, so that we contrast stops made in daylight and darkness on the same day of the week.

When we conduct the analysis, we do not find evidence of a racial bias in the decision to stop. Table 2.2 shows the results of the analysis over the five years of study, for all 598 stops in 2008 (shaded), and for the combined five years of the study (also shaded). The odds ratio indicates how many times more likely daylight stops are to involve a black driver than are stops in darkness.

In 2008, stops during daylight were slightly less likely than stops after dark to involve a black driver, which runs counter to the hypothesis of racial profiling, although there is considerable uncertainty in the estimate. More specifically, we estimate that the odds ratio is 0.83, suggesting that the odds of a daylight stop involving a black driver are lower than the odds that a stop after dark would involve a black driver, although the estimated 95-percent confidence interval ranges from 0.59 to 1.60. Looking across the years of analysis, we see that

---

[3] The logistic regression model outcome is an indicator of whether the driver was black, and the predictors include an indicator for darkness, clock time (separated into 12 discrete 15-minute intervals), and indicators for each day of the week.

Table 2.2
Comparison of the Odds of Black Versus Nonblack Drivers Being Stopped Between Daylight and Dark, Seasonally Focused

Year	Odds Ratio	95% Confidence Interval	p-Value	Number of Stops
2003	1.02	(0.70, 1.47)	0.93	543
2004	1.19	(0.80, 1.77)	0.37	465
2005	1.10	(0.81, 1.51)	0.53	763
2006	0.71	(0.51, 1.00)	0.05	606
2007	1.17	(0.87, 1.60)	0.29	751
2008	0.83	(0.59, 1.60)	0.26	598
Combined	0.96	(0.84, 1.11)	0.59	3,726

NOTE: Includes all stops occurring within 30 days of the spring or fall DST change during the evening intertwilight period.

the results are similar by year, with odds ratios being slightly greater in 2003, 2004, 2005, and 2007 and slightly less in 2006. *Combining across all six years indicates that there is no evidence of a racial bias in the decision to stop.*

In addition, the conclusion of no racial bias in the decision to stop is robust to additional adjustments for the neighborhood in which the stops take place.

As noted earlier, we conducted two analyses. The analysis summarized in Table 2.2 focuses on those stops in a tight period around the DST changes. That narrow focus aims to mitigate the risk that any observed differences might be the result of seasonal differences of drivers on the road rather than racial bias (e.g., the mix of black and nonblack drivers on the road in July may differ from the racial mix in December). Although we believe that the analysis is less prone to such errors, the price of that prudence is that we could use only 3,726 stops across five years. Large racial biases would be easily detected if they were present, but, if racial bias is not so pronounced, the analysis might not be sufficiently powerful to detect it.

So, as noted, we repeated the veil-of-darkness analysis using all stops occurring during the intertwilight period, regardless of when they occurred during the year. The result is a test that has less uncertainty—because it uses more stops—but is more sensitive to possible seasonal changes in the mix of black and nonblack drivers exposed to police.

Table 2.3 shows the results, which, again, indicate no evidence of racial profiling. As with the analysis of stops near DST, the 2008 odds ratio is less than 1.0, evidence that runs contrary to the existence of a racial bias against black drivers. The odds ratios in the second column are near 1.0 for all years, indicating that drivers have an equal chance of being stopped regardless of whether their races were visible in advance of the stop. Combining the analysis across all six years reinforces the conclusion of no racial bias in the decision to stop.

Table 2.3
Comparison of the Odds of Black Versus Nonblack Drivers Being Stopped Between Daylight and Dark, Year-Round

Year	Odds Ratio	95% Confidence Interval	p-Value	Number of Stops
2003	1.04	(0.90, 1.20)	0.55	3,899
2004	0.99	(0.87, 1.14)	0.94	4,346
2005[a]	1.06	(0.94, 1.20)	0.34	5,193
2006	0.90	(0.79, 1.02)	0.10	4,644
2007	0.94	(0.83, 1.05)	0.28	6,028
2008	0.84	(0.74, 0.95)	0.01	4,817
Combined	0.95	(0.90, 1.00)	0.04	28,927

NOTE: Includes all stops during the evening intertwilight period.

[a] The 2005 figures reported here differ slightly from those reported in the original analysis of the 2005 data (Ridgeway, Schell, Riley, et al., 2006), which double-counted observations. This did not affect the odds-ratio estimate—only the estimates of precision.

CHAPTER THREE

Do Individual Officers Appear to Have Racial Biases in Their Decisions to Stop?

Introduction

The veil-of-darkness analysis that we conducted and discussed in Chapter Two is intended to determine whether racial bias is a department-wide pattern of practice. As the results showed, when it comes to decisions to stop, we did not find a pattern of racial bias *across CPD as a whole*. However, it is still possible that there is racial bias in the decision to stop at the individual officer level. If problems are not CPD-wide, there still could be problems as a result of a few problem officers. In fact, such concerns about a few problem officers are consistent with prior research that has shown that a small fraction of police officers in a given department contribute to a disproportionate share of cases of abuse of authority (Sherman, 1978). If racial bias is the result of a few problem officers, the effect of their biases will likely not be large enough for the methods underlying the analysis in the previous chapter to detect the problem. And even if they somehow have the statistical power to detect the problem, they cannot help in identifying the potential problem officers.

In this chapter, we report on our analysis of whether there is racial bias in the decision to stop at the individual officer level. Doing so requires that we again use a benchmarking approach, but, in this case, we use an internal, as opposed to external, benchmark. This raises the question of how such an internal-benchmark approach should be designed. Walker (2001, 2002, 2003b) conceptualized an internal-benchmark method that compares officers' stop decisions with decisions made by other officers patrolling the same area at the same time, a comparison that is critical. Research notes that police-officer behavior varies as a function of location and time of the day and that those officers working in "troubled" areas with heavier workloads become more vigilant about intervening when a situation appears suspicious (Klinger, 1997). This, in turn, can skew the data, showing that certain officers stop more than others.

This basic internal-benchmark approach has been adopted as a part of several "early-warning systems" in identifying problem officers (Walker, 2003a). At the Los Angeles Police Department (LAPD), the Training Evaluation and Management System (TEAMS) II Risk Management Information System places officers in one of 33 peer groups (Birotte, 2007). Officers in the same peer group are presumably expected to conduct similar policing activities. If an officer exceeds certain thresholds compared with a peer group, such as being in the top 1 percent on number of complaints or number of use-of-force incidents, the system generates an action item for follow-up. However, officer roles in LAPD are certainly more diverse than 33 groups can capture, and the system generates more action items for potential problem officers than reasonably can be investigated. For example, an estimated 16 percent of the action items occurred after an officer had a single complaint or a single use-of-force incident, which means that the risk of false positives seems high. Similar problems are likely in other audit systems, like Pittsburgh's (Pa.) Performance Assessment and Review System and Phoenix's (Ariz.) Personnel Assessment System, which compute a peer officer–based formula to note officers (Walker, 2003a) but do not take into account the different environments in which officers in the same peer group work.

Given these concerns, we rely here on a method for constructing a customized internal benchmark for each officer, comparing the racial distribution of suspects stopped by the officer in question with the racial distribution of suspects stopped by other officers at the same times and places and in the same contexts. Rather than forming peer groups, our method creates a unique set of comparison stops for each officer, customized to the individual officer's unique assignment and patrol patterns. Specifically, we compare each officer to other officers who patrol the same neighborhoods at the same times and with the same assignment. This method selects an officer, identifies stops that other officers made at the same time and in the same neighborhood, and compares the racial distributions of the stopped drivers. Since the officers are patrolling the same areas at the same times, the racial distributions should be the same (assuming that the officers are on the same assignment). We report estimates of the percentage of officers who appear to stop drivers of one race disproportionately.[1]

We note that the analysis in this section offers an estimate of the number of CPD patrol officers of concern but that it does not identify the specific officers. All RAND studies go before an institutional review board (IRB) that reviews research involving human subjects, as required by federal regulations. RAND's Federalwide Assurance for the Protection of Human Subjects (DHHS, through 2011) serves as its assurance of compliance with the regulations of 16 federal departments and agencies. According to this assurance, the committee is responsible for review, regardless of funding source. These federal regulations prevent RAND research from singling out specific individuals whom its research could adversely affect, which, in this case, would be any officers identified in the analysis.

However, the point of such analysis is to highlight potential problem officers for further tracking. Thus, in the first quarter of 2007, RAND transferred capabilities to CPD analysts so that they could regularly run these analyses and conduct reviews of these officers. As a result, CPD now has the analytical capacity to replicate these analyses and complete more-extensive reporting on these cases. The system connects directly to CPD's contact-card database, constructs internal benchmarks for each officer, and produces a series of online reports navigable with a Web browser. These reports highlight those officers and include details on the stops included in the internal benchmark. These reports are now being included in the noted officers' quarterly reviews.

Our internal-benchmark analysis blends three modern statistical methodologies: propensity-score weighting, doubly robust estimation,

---

[1] See Fridell (2004, Chapter Eight) for an overview of internal benchmarking and its use in other jurisdictions.

and false-discovery rates. We use propensity-score weighting to construct each officer's internal benchmark, doubly robust estimation to remove any residual bias and reduce variance, and a false-discovery rate analysis to note potential problem officers. Ridgeway and MacDonald (2009) give complete details on the methodology. Appendixes A and B also provide brief overviews.

When we conduct the internal-benchmarking assessment, we find that, in 2008, *ten officers appear to be stopping significantly more black drivers than officers patrolling at the same times and places and in the same contexts.* The remainder of this chapter explains the approach we used and shows how this finding was derived.

What We Did

The fundamental goal of internal benchmarking here is to compare a particular officer's rate of stops of black drivers with the rate of stops of black drivers of other officers patrolling the same area at the same time. Matching in this way assures us that the target officer and the comparison officers are exposed to the same set of offenses and offenders.

Table 3.1 illustrates the matching process by presenting an internal benchmark constructed for a particular CPD officer based on the officer's stops; in this case, the officer had 111 stops, as shown in the shaded row at the top of the table. (The neighborhood codes have been scrambled to de-identify the officer.) We categorize those 111 stops in terms of the percentage of those that occurred by time, day, month, neighborhood, and reason for stop. For example, most of those stops occurred in neighborhood J (49 percent) and neighborhood K (33 percent), with some stops occurring elsewhere in the city. The final shaded row in the table shows the outcome on which we are focusing in our analysis: the percentage of those stops involving black drivers. As we can see, for Officer 534, 71 percent of these stops involved black drivers. Depending on the distribution of the races of drivers committing stoppable offenses whom this officer could have stopped, the 71 percent figure could be too high. If vehicle stops that other officers made in the same areas and times at which this officer's stops occurred involved

Table 3.1
Internal Benchmarking for an Example Officer: Officer 534

Variable		Stops Made by Officer 534 (%)	Similar Stops Made by Others (%)	
Number of stops		**111**	**571[b]**	**Effect Size[a]**
Time	12:00–4:00 p.m.	9	9	0.01
	4:00–8:00 p.m.	57	56	0.01
	8:00 p.m.–12:00 a.m.	34	35	−0.02
Day	Monday	20	20	0.00
	Tuesday	12	11	0.02
	Wednesday	12	12	−0.00
	Thursday	20	21	−0.03
	Friday	14	14	−0.01
	Saturday	11	11	−0.01
	Sunday	13	12	0.03
Month	January	12	12	0.01
	February	14	15	−0.02
	March	7	7	−0.01
	April	6	6	0.00
	May	8	7	0.05
	June	3	3	−0.03
	July	4	4	−0.02
	August	10	10	0.00
	September	6	6	0.03
	October	4	5	−0.03
	November	14	14	0.01
	December	11	11	−0.01

Table 3.1—Continued

Variable		Stops Made by Officer 534 (%)	Similar Stops Made by Others (%)	
Number of stops		**111**	**571[b]**	**Effect Size[a]**
Neighborhood[c]	H	1	1	−0.01
	I	1	1	−0.01
	J	49	48	0.02
	K	33	34	−0.02
	L	5	5	0.01
	M	11	11	−0.01
Stop reason	Equipment	64	63	0.01
	Moving	26	27	−0.01
	Other	10	10	−0.00
Outcome	Stops involving black drivers	71	46	

[a] The effect size is the difference of the two columns divided by the standard deviation of the first column. Generally, 0.20 is considered a small effect size, a value much larger than any effect size computed for this comparison.

[b] For the comparison stops, n represents the effective sample size.

[c] The neighborhoods have been given random letter codes to mask the officers' identities.

considerably less than 71 percent black drivers, further investigation of this officer is in order.

To internally benchmark Officer 534, we located 571 stops that collectively have the same distribution of stop features as the stops made by the officer in question, as shown in the table. They were made in the same places, at the same times, on the same days, during the same months, and for the same reasons. Since the officer made few stops in June and few in neighborhood H, the matched stops also showed very few stops in June and neighborhood H. Importantly, we created the matches without looking at the races of the drivers involved in the stops, mitigating the risk of setting up a comparison group of stops that would either absolve or fault the officer unfairly. Appendix A contains technical details about the matching methodology.

Of the matched stops, 46 percent involved a black driver, as shown at the bottom of the table. Officer 534 appears to have stopped a larger fraction of black drivers (71 percent) than did other officers making stops in the same area. Statistically speaking, this difference is larger than could be expected by chance. However, in a large collection of comparisons, some extreme differences can occur by chance.

The z-statistic is the commonly used statistical measure for assessing the magnitude of the difference between the percentage of an officer's stops involving a black driver and the officer's internal benchmark (Fridell, 2004). The z-statistic scales this difference to account for the number of stops that the officer made and the number of stops used to construct the internal benchmark, so that large differences based on a small number of stops are treated with greater uncertainty than large differences based on a large number of stops. Given the value of an officer's z-statistic, we can estimate the probability that a highlighted officer is, in fact, an outlier.

For our analysis here, we note all officers with an outlier probability exceeding 50 percent (equivalent in this analysis to a z-statistic cutoff of about 4.0). The choice of 50 percent as the cutoff is subjective and depends on the costs associated with failing to note a problem officer and those costs associated with investigating each noted officer. The use of a 50-percent cutoff implies that the cost of mistakenly noting an officer who is not an outlier equals the costs of failing to note an officer who is, in fact, an outlier. The commonly selected cutoff is 80 percent (Efron, 2004); however, the use of this higher level implies that mistakenly noting a good officer is four times more costly than failing to identify a problem officer, which may undervalue the cost of failing to do so.[2]

Different stakeholders may ascribe different costs to these failures. Some officers will bear the burden of being noted by chance even when they police no differently than their colleagues. Naturally, they

---

[2] Mathematically, an officer should be noted if his or her outlier probability exceeds (cost of noting a nonoutlier)/(cost of noting a nonoutlier + cost of failing to note a true outlier).

will assign high costs to the event of noting a good officer as an outlier. Black residents who interact most with the police would reasonably argue that the cost of interacting with a problem officer is exceedingly high and, therefore, even officers with a non-negligible probability of being an outlier should be scrutinized. Because of this subjectivity, the system that we have installed at CPD displays an outlier probability for each officer rather than providing hard classifications as "outlier" or "nonoutlier," leaving the subjective decision of where to draw the line to the user. Appendix B contains technical details about how we estimate the outlier probability.

For the analysis, we selected all CPD officers with more than 50 reported stops in 2008; 315 officers exceeded that cutoff. The 50-stop cutoff focuses the analysis on those officers most frequently interacting with drivers in Cincinnati. It also ensures having at least a minimum level of statistical power for detecting differences if they exist. These 315 officers amount to 44 percent of the CPD officers who reported a stop in 2008 and account for 90 percent of the 2008 stops.

What We Found

For the 315 officers with more than 50 reported stops in 2008, we created an internal benchmark for them, as we illustrated in Table 3.1. As such, stops were matched on month, day, time, neighborhood (53 neighborhoods plus nine highways and expressways), policing blocks (smaller partitions of a neighborhood) in which at least 10 percent of the officer's stops occurred, and the reason for the stop.

Table 3.2 summarizes the results of the analysis, listing ten officers with a greater-than-50-percent probability of having disproportionate stop patterns (the first and last columns of the table). The second and third columns in Table 3.2 indicate the number of stops made by the highlighted officer and that officer's internal benchmark. For example, highlighted Officer 1 made 116 stops in 2008, and we identified 1,554 stops to comprise the officer's benchmark that collectively had the same distribution of features as the highlighted officer's stops. The next two columns show the percentage of the officers' stops

Table 3.2
Summary of Internal-Benchmark Analysis

Officer	Number of Stops		Percentage of Stops Involving Black Driver		Probability Officer Exceeds the Benchmark
	Highlighted Officer	Internal Benchmark	Highlighted Officer	Internal Benchmark	
1	116	1,554	87	74	0.99
2	90	663	90	79	0.99
3	85	1,741	88	71	0.99
4	117	1,800	86	73	0.99
5	56	1,643	86	69	0.99
6	57	1,359	84	75	0.99
7	91	1,681	80	69	0.99
8	459	1,468	90	72	0.98
9	298	425	47	27	0.83
10	266	1,491	86	71	0.58

that involved a black driver compared to the officers' internal benchmark. Returning to the example, of highlighted Officer 1's 116 stops, 87 percent involved a black driver, while 74 percent of the 1,554 stops in the benchmark involved a black driver. The last column shows the estimated probability that the officer's stop patterns do, in fact, depart from other similarly situated stops. Based on highlighted Officer 1's stop pattern, for example, there is a 99-percent chance that this officer stops more black drivers than the other similarly situated officers do.

Using this analysis, we estimate that ten officers differ sufficiently from their internal benchmarks to warrant further investigation. At this stage, we do not know whether there is a problem with these officers or why we observe such large differences. These differences cannot be the result of differences in the stops' times, places, or reasons for stop, although some of these features are measured coarsely. These officers may have assignments that are targeted to very particular locations so that matching on neighborhood and policing block alone is insufficient.

CHAPTER FOUR

Are There Racial Disparities in the Outcomes of Stops?

Introduction

In the previous two chapters, we used the data on traffic stops from CPD to examine whether there was racial bias in the decision to stop at the department level and at the individual officer level. But once officers have made the decision to stop a motorist, there is also the possibility of racial bias or disparities in what happens after the stop—in the length of the stop, in the rates at which officers cite motorists, and in the way in which they conduct vehicle searches.

One way to look for the possibility of racial bias after stops is to analyze audio and video recordings from cameras mounted in CPD patrol cars that record what happens after stops, something that was done, as noted in Chapter One, during the first four years of the analysis. Such analyses were intended to shed light on the origins of police-community conflict and dissatisfaction, and the results of those analyses are presented in Ridgeway, Schell, Gifford, et al. (2009).

In the analyses discussed here, we use the traffic-stop data to get at the issue of whether there is racial bias in post-stop decisions for these outcomes. Specifically, we focus on post-stop outcomes, including the decision to cite and search and stop duration. We examine those traffic stops that did not involve arrest warrants, either in their initiation or conclusion. We used a method known as *propensity-score weighting* to identify stops involving nonblack drivers that are similarly situated to the stops involving black drivers and make post-stop comparisons between the two groups. Ridgeway (2006) gives a complete technical description of the method. Appendix A contains a brief overview.

When we conduct the propensity-score weighting analysis of post-stop decisions, we find the following:

- Black drivers who were stopped were slightly more likely to have their stops exceed 10 minutes, compared to similarly situated nonblack drivers.
- There was no racial difference in the percentage of stops lasting more than 30 minutes.
- Black drivers were less likely to receive citations than similarly situated nonblack drivers.
- Officers were less likely to conduct a high-discretion search, such as a consent search, of a black driver than of a similarly situated nonblack driver.
- When searched, black and nonblack drivers were equally likely to be found in possession of contraband.

The remainder of this chapter explains the approach we use and shows how these findings were derived.

What We Did

If we look at the raw numbers, officers conduct searches of 13 percent of stops involving black drivers, while the search rate for nonblack drivers is 6 percent. Regardless of whether a racial bias causes these differences, such differences can fuel the perception of racial bias, because they describe the differences in experiences of black and nonblack drivers in Cincinnati. Still, in focusing on whether racial bias did occur, we want to be able to tease out differences that might have arisen from racial bias relative to several other possible explanations that could apply. The methods we use here aim to isolate the effect of racial bias by measuring how much of the observed racial differences in search rates (and several other stop outcomes) can be explained by other factors.

Traffic stops involving black drivers occur at different times and places from those involving nonblack drivers. For example, 9 percent of stops involving black drivers occur in the Over-the-Rhine neighborhood, while 5 percent of stops of nonblack drivers occur there. At the same time, 29 percent of stops of nonblack drivers were made on the highways, while only 8 percent of stops of black drivers were made on the highways. In addition, the driver's sex and age, the number of passengers, where they live, and whether the driver has a valid license all differ by race. Moreover, these factors may, independent of race, influence an officer's post-stop decisionmaking process. For example, an officer may feel more (or less) compelled to issue a citation to a driver from Kentucky than to a Cincinnati resident. Since 11 percent of nonblack drivers stopped in Cincinnati have Kentucky license plates compared with only 2 percent of black drivers stopped in Cincinnati, apparent racial disparities in citation rates may result from differences in place of residence or other factors that are *associated* with race.

Whether these possible scenarios do, in fact, occur in the post-stop decisionmaking process, to ensure a fair comparison, we must match similarly situated black and nonblack drivers and compare their stop outcomes. Table 4.1 gives detailed information on stop features by driver race across a series of features: neighborhood, place of residence, reason for stop, time of day of stop, state of vehicle registration, number and age of occupants in vehicle, day and month of stop, and percentage male. The fact that the table is as long as it is reflects all the features that could account for racial bias that need to be adjusted using the propensity-score weighting approach.

Table 4.1
Features of Stops Involving Black and Nonblack Drivers, Matched and Unmatched

Stop Features	Black Drivers (%) (n = 26,941)	Matched Nonblack Drivers (%) (n = 4,952)	Nonblack Drivers (%) (n = 25,149)
Neighborhood			
CBD and Riverfront	1.8	1.8	4.1
Queensgate	0.7	0.7	1.4
West End	4.7	4.5	1.9
Over-the-Rhine	9.3	10.1	4.7

Table 4.1—Continued

Stop Features	Black Drivers (%) (n = 26,941)	Matched Nonblack Drivers (%) (n = 4,952)	Nonblack Drivers (%) (n = 25,149)
Mount Adams	0.2	0.2	0.9
Pendleton	0.5	0.4	0.2
East End	0.8	0.6	1.9
East Walnut Hills	0.6	0.5	0.7
Evanston	3.7	3.1	0.9
Hyde Park	0.4	0.4	1.7
Oakley	0.5	0.6	1.4
O'Bryonville	0.1	0.1	0.2
Pleasant Ridge	0.9	0.9	0.5
Kennedy Heights	0.6	0.5	0.2
Mount Lookout	0.1	0.1	0.6
Columbia/Tusculum	0.2	0.2	1.2
Linwood	0.1	0.1	0.5
Madisonville	1.7	1.6	1.2
Mount Washington	0.2	0.2	1.4
Sayler Park	0.0	0.0	0.4
Riverside	0.1	0.1	1.8
Sedamsville	0.3	0.3	2.5
North Fairmount	0.8	0.8	0.3
English Woods	0.4	0.4	0.1
East Westwood	1.2	1.3	0.3
Millvale	1.7	1.6	0.5
Fay Apartments	1.1	1.1	0.1
South Cumminsville	0.7	0.6	0.2
East Price Hill	3.1	3.4	3.1

Table 4.1—Continued

Stop Features	Black Drivers (%) (n = 26,941)	Matched Nonblack Drivers (%) (n = 4,952)	Nonblack Drivers (%) (n = 25,149)
West Price Hill	1.9	2.1	3.8
Westwood	4.5	4.7	4.0
Lower Price Hill	0.9	1.0	3.0
South Fairmount	4.8	5.2	2.6
Mount Auburn	1.3	1.1	0.8
Corryville	1.9	1.9	1.1
Avondale	5.0	4.5	1.0
North Avondale	2.2	1.9	0.5
Paddock Hills	0.8	0.7	0.2
Hartwell	0.4	0.4	0.5
Carthage	0.7	0.7	0.7
Roselawn	1.6	1.4	0.5
Bond Hill	2.5	2.2	0.6
Walnut Hills	4.7	4.6	2.4
College Hill	3.7	3.4	0.8
Clifton and University Heights	2.1	2.3	2.5
Fairview	1.8	2.0	2.0
Northside	4.4	4.5	2.3
Clifton	2.2	2.2	2.8
Mount Airy	3.3	3.3	1.3
Winton Hills	1.4	1.0	0.1
Winton Place	1.7	1.8	0.8
Camp Washington	1.6	1.8	1.3
I-275	0.0	0.0	0.5

Table 4.1—Continued

Stop Features	Black Drivers (%) (n = 26,941)	Matched Nonblack Drivers (%) (n = 4,952)	Nonblack Drivers (%) (n = 25,149)
I-471	0.0	0.0	0.1
I-71	2.3	2.7	10.9
I-74	0.9	1.0	4.9
I-75	4.3	4.9	11.4
Red Bank Expressway	0.1	0.1	0.3
Ronald Reagan Highway	0.0	0.0	0.0
Sixth Street Expressway	0.2	0.2	1.1
SR-562	0.1	0.1	0.2
Place of residence			
Cincinnati	93.0	92.4	60.8
Ohio (not Cincinnati)	3.7	4.0	19.9
Kentucky	0.3	0.3	0.9
Outside Ohio and Kentucky	3.0	3.3	18.4
Reason for stop			
Equipment violation	27.3	28.0	16.3
Moving violation	51.4	52.3	76.3
Offense	2.4	2.1	0.8
Other	8.7	8.5	3.1
Stolen auto	0.3	0.3	0.1
Suspect in vehicle	9.9	8.7	3.4
Invalid driver's license (%)			
	21.8	20.1	7.2

Table 4.1—Continued

Stop Features	Black Drivers (%) (n = 26,941)	Matched Nonblack Drivers (%) (n = 4,952)	Nonblack Drivers (%) (n = 25,149)
Time of day of stop			
12:00–3:00 a.m.	20.2	20.1	14.5
3:00–6:00 a.m.	4.1	4.2	3.2
6:00–9:00 a.m.	4.4	4.5	9.3
9:00 a.m.–12:00 p.m.	6.5	6.8	13.4
12:00–3:00 p.m.	7.1	6.9	10.8
3:00–6:00 p.m.	19.6	19.6	17.2
6:00–9:00 p.m.	18.6	17.6	14.6
9:00 p.m.–12:00 a.m.	19.6	20.2	17.0
State of car registration			
Ohio	95.2	94.9	81.9
Kentucky	2.4	2.3	11.1
Other	2.4	2.8	7.0
Number of occupants in vehicle			
1	58.7	58.4	69.6
2	26.7	27.8	20.7
3	9.1	9.0	6.0
4	3.9	3.7	2.9
>4	1.5	1.1	0.8
Age of occupants in vehicle (years)			
0–17	1.4	1.1	1.5
18–25	33.4	31.7	28.6
26–35	29.0	29.2	26.7
36–45	18.1	19.2	19.3
46+	18.2	18.8	23.9

Table 4.1—Continued

Stop Features	Black Drivers (%) (n = 26,941)	Matched Nonblack Drivers (%) (n = 4,952)	Nonblack Drivers (%) (n = 25,149)
Day of week stop occurred			
Monday	14.5	14.9	13.5
Tuesday	15.4	15.2	15.0
Wednesday	15.0	14.7	14.8
Thursday	15.0	15.2	15.8
Friday	14.7	14.6	15.3
Saturday	14.2	14.3	15.0
Sunday	11.1	11.1	10.6
Month stop occurred			
January	9.7	9.8	8.3
February	9.1	8.7	8.0
March	8.3	8.6	7.5
April	9.9	9.9	10.6
May	9.5	8.9	9.2
June	8.4	8.8	8.1
July	8.4	7.9	8.7
August	8.6	9.4	11.2
September	7.0	6.5	7.7
October	6.9	7.3	7.7
November	7.1	7.6	6.9
December	6.9	6.6	6.2
Male (%)			
	65.1	65.0	65.9

NOTE: Stops were matched also by policing blocks within each neighborhood. Policing blocks divide the 53 neighborhoods into a total of 509 smaller regions. CBD = Central Business District.

The Black Drivers column shows the distribution of stop features involving black drivers. The Nonblack Drivers column shows the same distribution for all stops involving nonblack drivers. Comparisons between these two columns show large differences. The shaded rows mark a few of the particularly large differences across the features. As part of the propensity-score weighting approach, we need to create a set of nonblack drivers who are matched relative to the black drivers on these features. If we look at the resulting Matched Nonblack Drivers column, we see that it is nearly identical to the Black Drivers column. Arriving at this near match on the distribution of stop features required effectively paring the set of stops of nonblack drivers down from 25,149 to 4,952. This process downweighted and, at times, removed stops of nonblack drivers that had features that were atypical of stops involving black drivers. The key point of Table 4.1 is that any differences between black drivers and the matched nonblack drivers that we observe in post-stop outcomes *cannot* be the result of any of the factors listed in Table 4.1. To isolate the effect of a racial bias, we must adjust for all factors associated with both race and post-stop outcomes, and we have made a concerted effort to include all such observable features in this analysis.

While we attempted to account for as many stop features as possible that might be associated with both race and stop outcomes, it is plausible that other variables not listed in Table 4.1 might be important. For example, the contact cards give no information on how serious the moving violations were. If one racial group committed more-serious or more-dangerous moving violations, our matching cannot account for this. Differences in stop outcomes between black and matched nonblack drivers may be the result of racial bias or any unobserved factor not listed in Table 4.1, such as seriousness of offense.

Still, given the extensive list of factors in Table 4.1, we can be fairly certain that we have covered most of the likely sources of variables that could lead to the differences in the stops of black and nonblack drivers other than racial bias. Using the matching process shown in Table 4.1, we can determine the factors that most distinguish their stops: how much each of the factors contributed to eliminating the differences between the two groups.

It turns out that most of the difference between the features of stops of black and nonblack drivers involves differences in stop locations (67 percent). Driver residence was also an important factor on which the black and nonblack driver stops greatly differed (21 percent). Reason for stop, invalid driver's license, time of stop, driver sex, number of vehicle occupants, state of license-plate registration, age of driver, and day and month of stop accounted for the remaining 12 percent.

What We Found

As mentioned earlier, we are interested in determining whether racial bias exists in post-stop outcomes—in particular, stop duration, citation rates, search rates, and hit rates. We present the results here for 2008 and for all the previous years of the analyses. To keep the discussion more accessible in the main document, we summarize key results in a series of simple graphics; the complete analysis results can be found in a series of tables in Appendix C.

Stop Duration

One of the post-stop outcomes we want to analyze is how long the actual stop took. The stop-duration analyses were adjusted for all the factors listed in Table 4.1, as well as for whether the officer issued a citation, conducted an arrest, and performed a search. Thus, any differences in stop duration cannot be attributed to citations, arrests, searches, or any of the factors listed in the table.

Figure 4.1 shows the stop durations for black and nonblack drivers, focusing here on those stops lasting between 0 and 10 minutes. (Table C.1 in Appendix C shows more-detailed results.) For 2008 data, we find that black drivers were less likely to have stops lasting less than 10 minutes than nonblack drivers who are not matched (55 versus 65 percent); however, that difference reflects a comparison of stops between black drivers and unmatched nonblack drivers.

When we compare black to similarly situated nonblack drivers—that is, use the propensity-score approach to account for the factors in Table 4.1—the difference is substantially reduced, from a 10-percentage-

Figure 4.1
Stop Durations of Black and Nonblack Drivers, 0–10 Minutes, 2003–2008

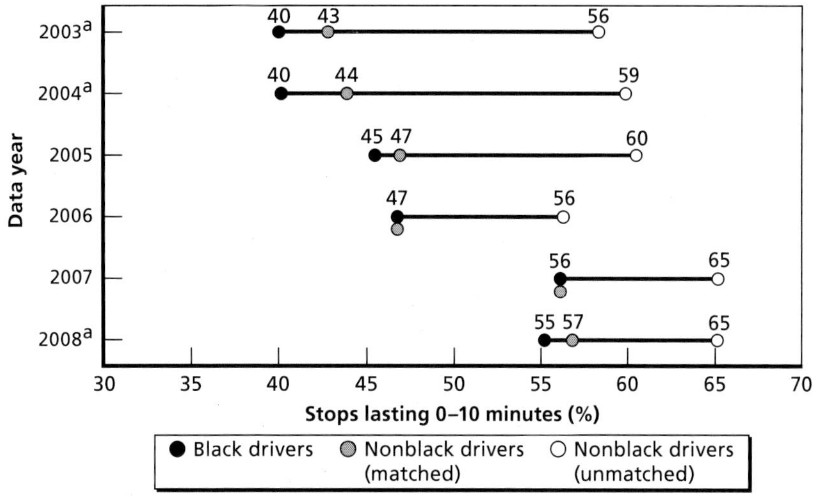

[a] We find statistically significant differences between the rates for black drivers and the rates for matched nonblack drivers.
RAND *MG914-4.1*

point difference (55 percent versus 65 percent) to a 2-percentage-point difference (55 percent versus 57 percent), as shown in the figure. Thus, the difference between 65 and 55 percent is largely the result of differences in stop location, the driver's residency, the validity of driver's license, and other factors (e.g., highway traffic stops may take less time than other traffic stops). As a result, the places, times, and conditions under which officers stopped black drivers tended to influence the length of the stops. Nonblack drivers stopped under those same conditions had nearly the same stop durations.

Citation Rates

In addition to determining whether the duration of the stop varies by the race of the driver, we also want to know whether the rate at which police give citations after a stop varies by the driver's race. Figure 4.2 compares citation rates for black drivers with those for a matched set of nonblack drivers. (Table C.2 in Appendix C contains more-detailed statistics about the citation rates.) Stops initiated because of an arrest

Figure 4.2
Citation Rates of Black and Nonblack Drivers, 2003–2008

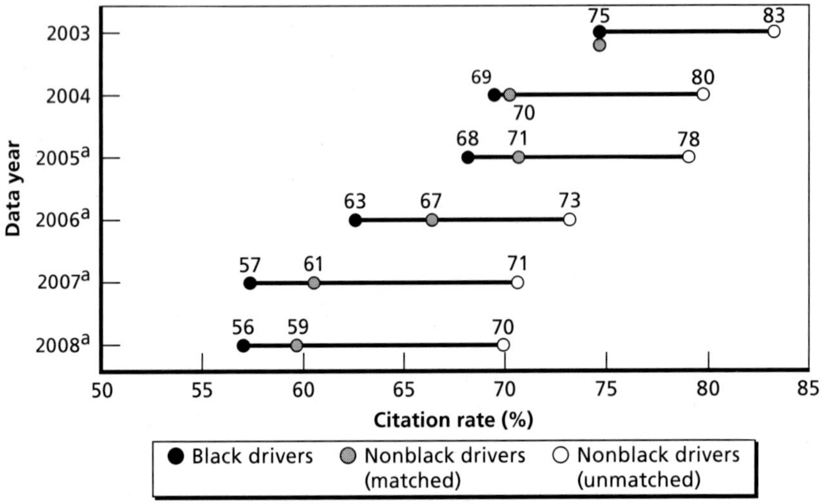

[a] We found statistically significant differences between the rates for black and matched nonblack drivers.

RAND *MG914-4.2*

warrant or concluding with an arrest because of an outstanding warrant were excluded from this analysis.

As the leftward shift of the lines over the years in Figure 4.2 shows, citation rates as a whole have generally been decreasing over the past five years. During this period, there was also a push to document all traffic stops including the use of CAD records to audit officers' completion of contact cards. Therefore, this apparent decline is more likely a result of CPD's data-quality improvements and the high rate of compliance even for stops that do not result in citations. In 2003 and 2004, the citation rates for black and matched nonblack drivers were essentially the same. But since 2005 (as we can see in the figure), we have found a 3- to 4-percentage-point gap between the citation rates for black and matched nonblack drivers. Statistically, this is a significant difference. A 3-percent gap may not be negligible. We do not expect all stops to result in citations, and we expect some number of investigatory stops. However, one interpretation of the 3-percent gap is that police stopped in excess of 800 black drivers (3 percent of 27,000 stops). An alternative explanation is that the black drivers who would have received citations were among those found to have outstanding warrants and were arrested rather than cited.

Search

The decision to search involves many factors and different levels of officer discretion. If a search occurred, the contact card included the legal basis for the search. We coded the following legal bases as high discretion: consent, reasonable suspicion of weapon, dog alert, odor (alcohol or drugs), and other probable cause. We coded the following legal bases as low discretion: plain view, inventory, and incident to arrest. High-discretion searches are the searches most at risk for racial bias, so we focus on those here.

Figure 4.3 compares adjusted and unadjusted search rates for high-discretion searches over the five years. (Table C.3 in Appendix C shows the breakdown for high, low, and all searches over the five years.) From 2003 through 2005, we see a similar pattern to what

Figure 4.3
Rates of High-Discretion Searches, 2003–2008

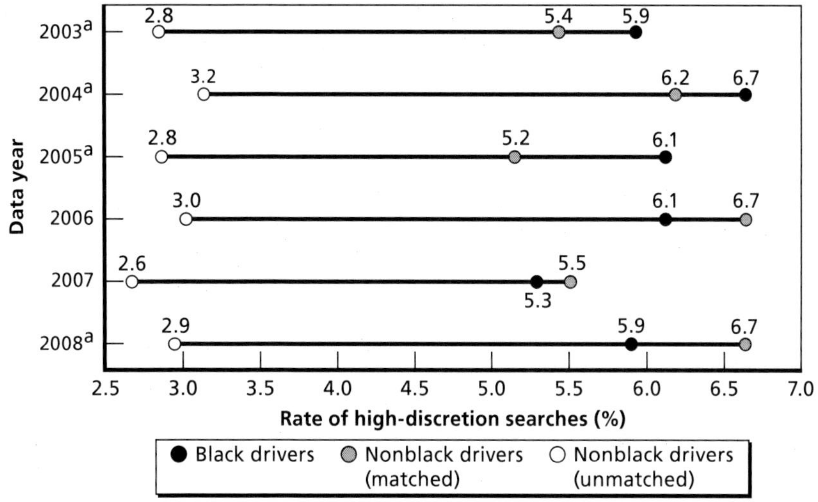

[a] We found statistically significant differences between the rates for black and matched nonblack drivers.

RAND *MG914-4.3*

we saw in the previous post-stop outcomes: Black drivers are more likely than unmatched nonblack drivers to undergo high-discretion searches, but that difference diminishes when we account for other factors. However, from 2006 on, we see that officers are actually *less* likely to search black drivers relative to matched nonblack drivers, as shown by the shift in the position of the black and gray dots. In 2008, high-discretion searches occurred in 5.9 percent of stops of black drivers while the rate is 6.7 percent for similarly situated nonblack drivers. While the search rate of black motorists is twice the citywide search rate of all nonblack motorists (2.9 percent of stops of nonblack drivers involve high-discretion searches), after taking into account important factors (e.g., time and location of stop, whether the motorist has a valid driver's license), the search rates of nonblack drivers slightly exceed the search rate of black drivers.

It is important to note that the unmatched analysis shows that there are large differences in the experiences that black and nonblack drivers have: 5.9 percent versus 2.9 percent, respectively, in 2008. And when we look across all searches (shown in Table C.3 in Appendix C) for 2008, we see that officers search black drivers at a rate that is more than double the rate for nonblack drivers (13.1 percent versus 6.3 percent). These differences in experiences can differentially shape black drivers' views of CPD officers. Our analysis indicates that factors other than racial bias can explain much of these differences; black drivers are stopped in locations, times, and situations for which officers are much more likely to search (e.g., in neighborhoods with more crime, such as Over-the-Rhine). Nonblack drivers stopped in those situations are equally likely to be searched, so individual officer racial bias cannot be the reason for the observed difference in search rates. Nonetheless, this will be of little solace to the many searched black drivers, even if all the searches were legitimate and conducted professionally.

When we look at consent searches—the highest-discretion searches—we see the same pattern (Figure 4.4). (Table C.4 in Appendix C breaks down the searches in more detail from highest to lowest discretion across the years.) As we saw with all high-discretion searches, in recent years (from 2005 on), stops involving black drivers are *less* likely to involve a search based on consent. However, stops of black

Figure 4.4
Rates of Consent Searches, 2003–2008

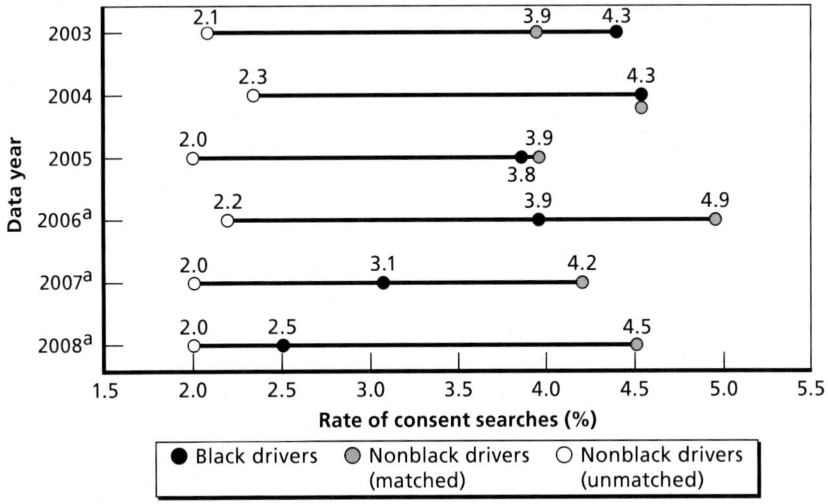

[a] We found statistically significant differences between the rates for black and matched nonblack drivers.

RAND *MG914-4.4*

drivers are more likely than stops of nonblack drivers to involve a search based on reasonable suspicion of a weapon (shown in Table C.4 in Appendix C). These two are not unrelated. Unless the officer believes that there is reasonable suspicion of a weapon, that officer would not necessarily pursue a consent search.

Again, we stress that comparisons with unmatched nonblack drivers exaggerate the search-rate disparity, conflating potential racial bias with circumstances surrounding the stop. When they are properly matched, we found that black and nonblack drivers stopped under the same conditions had more-similar search rates.

In addition, as noted in our previous reports, police search practices put the greatest burden of search on stop conditions that were more common to black drivers. As a result, Cincinnati's black residents were more likely to be stopped under conditions that elevated the chance of a search (e.g., driving in a high-crime neighborhood). Some characteristics, such as having a valid driver's license, are clearly in the driver's hands. Officers searched 26 percent of the drivers stopped without a license, regardless of race. However, stopped black drivers were more than three times more likely than were nonblack drivers to have an invalid driver's license (22 percent versus 7 percent), greatly increasing the prevalence of searches among black drivers.

Hit Rates

A search's success depends partially on whether contraband is found (Ayres, 2002). If police searched more drivers, their hit rates (the rate at which they recovered contraband) would likely decrease, because they would be searching drivers who are less suspicious. If the hit rates were lower for one racial group, this would suggest that officers searched that racial group more often than they did other racial groups.

Table 4.2 separates hit rates by level of discretion. We classify high-discretion searches as those conducted with consent, for reasonable suspicion of a weapon, dog alert, alcohol or drug odor, or other probable cause. Low-discretion searches include searches because of contraband in plain view, inventory searches, and searches incident to arrest. The number of reported searches continues to increase; 2007 and 2008 show a 5-percent increase in searches over 2006 (which already had a 16-percent increase over 2005). A 13-percent increase in low-discretion searches, such as searches incident to arrest, led to the increase.

For high-discretion searches (the bolded and shaded rows in the table), the hit rates for black drivers are nearly the same as the hit rates for nonblack drivers. *The similarity of these rates suggests that racial bias does not play a role in officers' selection of which drivers to search.* The hit rates have varied over time but, importantly, do not seem to be related to the number of searches. That is, the doubling of the number of high-discretion searches between 2003 and 2005 did not result in a decrease in the hit rate. The 2007 hit rate was the lowest of any during the study period.

Even though we found no racial bias, officers conducted 1,324 high-discretion searches of black drivers in 2008 that recovered no contraband. Such stops, which the motorist likely views as being made for no good reason, disproportionately affect the black community and likely contribute to blacks' perceptions of unfair policing that were identified in last year's report (Ridgeway, Schell, Gifford, et al., 2009).

Table 4.2
Hit Rates, by Year and Race

		Black Drivers		Nonblack Drivers		
Year	Discretion	Number of Searches	Hit Rate (%)	Number of Searches	Hit Rate (%)	p-Value
2003	High	982	28.0	517	22.4	0.02
	Low	1,360	16.3	495	16.2	0.96
2004	High	1,250	28.8	649	26.7	0.35
	Low	1,984	19.4	798	20.8	0.43
2005	High	1,743	29.0	1,011	26.5	0.18
	Low	2,763	19.6	1,203	15.5	0.00
2006	High	1,858	23.3	1,023	23.6	0.91
	Low	3,654	21.5	1,582	21.0	0.75
2007	High	1,642	19.7	835	20.5	0.70
	Low	4,130	18.3	1,689	20.1	0.13
2008	High	1,684	21.4	780	20.0	0.47
	Low	4,109	20.6	1,620	21.6	0.44

NOTE: The number of searches may not equal the total searches because officers did not record the legal basis for some of the searches.

While recovery of contraband from high-discretion searches, such as 33 weapon and 474 drug recoveries, can have a social benefit for the Cincinnati community, there is a societal cost for searches that result in no recovery of contraband.

CHAPTER FIVE

Conclusions and Implications

In 2008, RAND researchers completed a comprehensive assessment of the impact of the collaborative agreement on police-community relations in Cincinnati (Ridgeway, Schell, Gifford, et al., 2009). Researchers conducted multiple tasks to assess the impact of that agreement, directly surveying the residents of Cincinnati, analyzing data on interactions between the police and citizens, and documenting the actions and communication quality observed in video recordings of traffic stops.

When RAND was first engaged to assess progress toward the goals of the collaborative agreement, racial disparities in traffic stops were viewed as key point of concern. As a result, RAND has analyzed data on all traffic stops that Cincinnati police officers have documented since 2003. In addition, while all other major tasks previously listed in Chapter One were finalized in 2008, the parties to the collaborative agreement asked that we also analyze 2008 traffic-stop data in a separate report, the results of which are presented here.

In analyzing the 2008 data, as in analyzing the data in recent years, we found that, in similar circumstances, black and nonblack drivers have similar stop outcomes. They have an equal chance of being searched, an equal chance of having a short traffic stop, a smaller chance of receiving a citation, and, when searched, an equal chance of being found with contraband. We also found no evidence of a department-wide pattern of racial bias in the decision to make stops. These findings endorse the collaborative agreement's goal of "ensuring fair and equitable treatment for all members of the community."

Although we found no evidence of racial differences between the stops of black and similarly situated nonblack drivers, there are issues that can exacerbate the perception of racial bias. First, in each year of analysis, we find several officers who stop substantially more black drivers than their peers stop. These represent a small fraction of CPD officers, and, as noted earlier, CPD has the capability to monitor, manage, and address issues that these officers may present to the department and the community. Second, although black and similarly situated nonblack drivers have similar stop outcomes, the burden of policing falls disproportionately on black residents.

There are still substantial gaps between how black and nonblack residents view CPD. As noted in last year's report (Ridgeway, Schell, Gifford, et al., 2009), the improvements that have been seen over the life of the collaborative agreement may be fragile. It will require a continued and concerted effort on the part of CPD and community leaders to maintain progress toward the goals stated in the collaborative agreement, as well as to prevent reversals in the positive trends that we observed while this agreement was in force.

APPENDIX A

Details of the Propensity-Score Weighting Approach

In this appendix, we briefly describe the propensity-score weighting approach that underlies analyses presented in the main document.

We used propensity-score weighting to reweight stops from a comparison group to have the same distribution of features as the stops in a reference group. The choice of reference and comparison groups differs by the analytical question being addressed. For the internal-benchmark analysis, the reference stops are those that the officer in question made, while the comparison stops are the stops that other officers made. For the post-stop analysis, the reference stops are those involving a black driver, while the comparison stops are those involving a nonblack driver.

Stops in the comparison group are weighted. No stops are explicitly excluded from the sample, but some may receive very small weights. The weights are constructed in such a way that any weighted statistic of the comparison group (e.g., weighted average age, weighted percentage from neighborhood A, weighted percentage stopped between midnight and 4:00 a.m.) will match the same unweighted statistic computed for the reference group.

Let $\mathbf{x}$ represent the collection of stop features and t be a binary indicator that the stop is a member of the reference group. The distribution $f(\mathbf{x}|t=1)$ represents the conditional distribution of stop features for those stops in the reference group, and $f(\mathbf{x}|t=0)$ represents the distribution of features for stops in the comparison group. We want to weight the comparison group's distribution, $f(\mathbf{x}|t=0)$, so that

$$f(\mathbf{x}|t=1) = w(\mathbf{x})\, f(\mathbf{x}|t=0),$$

where $w(\mathbf{x})$ is the weighting function of interest to us. Solving for $w(\mathbf{x})$ and applying Bayes' theorem to the numerator and denominator yields

$$w(\mathbf{x}) = K f(t=1|\mathbf{x})/f(t=0|\mathbf{x})$$

where K is a constant that will later drop out of the analysis. The right side of the expression is proportional to the probability that a stop with feature $\mathbf{x}$ is in the reference group divided by the probability that a stop with feature $\mathbf{x}$ is in the comparison group.

This indicates that, for a comparison-group stop with feature $\mathbf{x}$, we should apply a weight equal to the odds that a stop with feature $\mathbf{x}$ was in the reference group. Note that, if reference-group stops rarely occur in neighborhood A, for example, then all comparison-group stops made in neighborhood A will receive a weight near 0. On the other hand, comparison-group stops with features much like those of the reference group's will receive large weights.

To estimate $f(t=1|\mathbf{x})$, we use a nonparametric version of logistic regression. See McCaffrey, Ridgeway, and Morral (2004) or Ridgeway (2006) for complete details. We evaluate the quality of the weights by how well the distribution of the features matches between the reference group and the weighted stops in the comparison group.

APPENDIX B

Estimating False-Discovery Rates

In this appendix, we briefly discuss the approach we used in estimating false-discovery rates.

Fridell (2004) notes that a popular statistic for measuring the difference between an officer's minority-stop fraction and the officer's internal benchmark is the z-statistic,

$$z = \frac{p_t - p_c}{\sqrt{\frac{p_t(1-p_t)}{N_t} + \frac{p_c(1-p_c)}{N_c}}}. \qquad \text{B.1}$$

In this measure, p_t and p_c are, respectively, the proportion of stops involving black drivers for the target and the weighted comparison stops. The denominator normalizes this term to have variance 1. This statistic is computed for all officers under consideration. In standard circumstances, z will have a standard normal distribution, and there will be a 5-percent probability that the absolute value of z exceeds 2.0 when there is no difference between the officer's stop rate and the internal benchmark. However, in a collection of 294 *independent* comparisons with no racial bias, we should expect about 15 officers (5 percent of 294) to have z-statistics exceeding 2.0 by chance. Thus, highlighting or noting officers with z exceeding 2.0 is bound to select officers with no racial biases. Further complicating matters is that the 294 z-statistics are *not* independent. They are correlated with each other, since each officer might be used in another officer's internal benchmark. In this case, the empirical distribution of the z's may be much wider (or narrower) than would be predicted by statistical theory (Efron, 2005).

Benjamini and Hochberg (1995) pioneered the use of the false-discovery rate (fdr) as an alternative methodology for locating truly extreme values in multiple comparison situations. The fdr is the probability of no group difference given the value of an observed test statistic, z (Efron, 2004).

We can derive the probability of an officer being an outlier as

$$\begin{aligned} P(\text{outlier} \mid z) &= 1 - P(\text{not outlier} \mid z) \\ &= 1 - \frac{f(z \mid \text{not outlier})\, f(\text{not outlier})}{f(z)} \\ &\geq 1 - \frac{f_0(z)}{f(z)}, \end{aligned} \qquad \text{B.2}$$

where $f_0(z)$ is the distribution of z for nonoutlier officers and $f(z)$ is the distribution of z for all officers (Efron, 2004). If the fraction of problem officers is small (less than 10 percent), the bound in the last line of Equation B.2 is near equality. We estimate $f_0(z)$ with the empirical null, assuming normal distribution but with location and variance estimated using only the central data of the distribution.

We used the R package locfdr 1.1-6 (Efron, Turnbull, and Narasimhan, 2007) for this analysis' calculations.

APPENDIX C

Detailed Tables for Post-Stop Outcomes

In this appendix, we present the detailed results in table form for the analyses of post-stop outcomes documented in Chapter Four, including stop durations (Table C.1), citation rates (Table C.2), and search rates (Tables C.3 and C.4).

Table C.1
Stop Durations for Black and Nonblack Drivers

Year	Stop Duration (Minutes)	Black Drivers (%)	Nonblack Drivers (%) Matched	Nonblack Drivers (%) Unmatched
2003[a]		n = 16,708	n = 4,881	n = 18,548
	[0, 10]	40	43	56
	(10, 20]	42	41	36
	(20, 30]	10	9	5
	(30, 360]	8	7	4
2004[a]		n = 18,721	n = 5,190	n = 20,390
	[0, 10]	40	44	59
	(10, 20]	43	39	33
	(20, 30]	10	10	5
	(30, 360]	8	7	3

Table C.1—Continued

Year	Stop Duration (Minutes)	Black Drivers (%)	Nonblack Drivers (%)	
			Matched	Unmatched
2005[b,c]		n = 15,571	n = 4,965	n = 20,431
	[0, 10]	45	47	60
	(10, 20]	43	42	34
	(20, 30]	7	7	4
	(30, 360]	4	4	2
2006[d]		n = 15,557	n = 3,358	n = 18,458
	[0, 10]	47	47	56
	(10, 20]	42	40	35
	(20, 30]	8	8	6
	(30, 360]	4	5	2
2007[c]		n = 22,406	n = 4,963	n = 24,142
	[0, 10]	56	56	65
	(10, 20]	35	34	29
	(20, 30]	6	7	5
	(30, 360]	3	3	2
2008[a]		n = 26,891	n = 4,674	n = 25,072
	[0, 10]	55	57	65
	(10, 20]	35	34	28
	(20, 30]	6	7	5
	(30, 360]	3	3	2

[a] In 2003, 2004, and 2008, there was a significant difference in the distribution of stop durations between black and nonblack drivers.

[b] This analysis excludes stops with missing stop durations, which comprised about 20 percent of the 2005 stops and 24 percent of the 2006 stops.

[c] In 2005 and 2007, there was no significant difference in the distribution of stop durations between black and similarly situated nonblack drivers.

[d] In 2006, black drivers were significantly less likely to have stops exceeding 30 minutes than were similarly situated nonblack drivers.

Table C.2
Citation Rates of Black Drivers and of a Matched Set of Nonblack Drivers

		Nonblack Drivers		
Year	Black Drivers	Matched	Unmatched	p-Value
2003	n = 12,064	n = 4,438	n = 16,318	0.98
	74.6%	74.6%	82.7%	
2004	n = 12,507	n = 4,386	n = 16,920	0.14
	69.2%	70.4%	79.9%	
2005	n = 19,375	n = 6,141	n = 25,163	< 0.001
	67.7%	70.8%	78.1%	
2006	n = 20,146	n = 5,365	n = 24,383	< 0.001
	62.7%	66.5%	73.3%	
2007	n = 22,479	n = 4,996	n = 24,220	< 0.001
	57.1%	60.5%	70.7%	
2008	n = 26,941	n = 4,952	n=25,149	<0.001
	56.3%	59.3%	69.7%	

NOTE: The shaded cells indicate the most-relevant comparisons.

Table C.3
Searches of Black Drivers and of a Matched Set of Nonblack Drivers

			Nonblack Drivers (%)		
Year	Discretion	Black Drivers	Matched (%)	Unmatched	p-Value
2003		n = 16,708	n = 4,992	n = 18,548	
	High	5.9	5.4	2.8	0.00
	Low	8.1	5.5	2.7	0.00
	All	14.0	10.9	5.5	0.00

Table C.3—Continued

Year	Discretion	Black Drivers	Nonblack Drivers (%)		p-Value
			Matched (%)	Unmatched	
2004		n = 18,721	n = 5,342	n = 20,390	
	High	6.7	6.2	3.2	0.00
	Low	10.7	7.0	3.9	0.00
	All	17.4	13.2	7.1	0.00
2005		n = 19,375	n = 6,141	n = 25,163	
	High	6.1	5.2	2.8	0.00
	Low	4.4	3.5	1.6	0.00
	All	11.4	9.4	4.7	0.00
2006		n = 20,146	n = 5,365	n = 24,383	
	High	6.1	6.7	3.0	0.06
	Low	4.9	3.9	1.8	0.04
	All	11.0	10.7	4.8	0.82
2007		n = 22,479	n = 4,996	n = 24,220	
	High	5.3	5.5	2.6	0.52
	Low	4.9	5.2	1.9	0.43
	All	10.6	10.9	4.7	0.44
2008		n = 26,941	n = 4,952	n = 25,149	
	High	5.9	6.7	2.9	0.04
	Low	7.1	7.4	3.4	0.48
	All	13.1	14.3	6.3	0.04

NOTE: The shaded cells indicate the most-relevant comparison, comparing black drivers to matched nonblack drivers on high-discretion searches.

Table C.4
Detailed Comparison of Searches of Stopped Black Drivers with Those of a Matched Set of Nonblack Drivers

Year	Legal Basis (sorted roughly from high to low discretion)	Black Drivers (%)	Nonblack Drivers (%)		p-Value
			Matched	Unmatched	
2003		n = 16,708	n = 4,992	n = 18,548	
	Consent	4.3	3.9	2.1	0.35
	Reasonable suspicion of weapon	0.4	0.3	0.1	0.54
	Dog alert	0.0	0.0	0.0	0.76
	Odor (alcohol or drugs)	0.9	0.8	0.5	0.00
	Other probable cause	0.4	0.4	0.2	0.94
	Plain view	0.4	0.3	0.2	0.17
	Inventory	0.7	0.5	0.2	0.11
	Incident to arrest	7.0	4.8	2.4	0.00
2004		n = 18,721	n = 5,342	n = 20,390	
	Consent	4.5	4.5	2.3	0.83
	Reasonable suspicion of weapon	0.5	0.4	0.2	0.25
	Dog alert	0.2	0.0	0.0	0.12
	Odor (alcohol or drugs)	1.1	0.6	0.4	0.00
	Other probable cause	0.6	0.6	0.3	0.91
	Plain view	0.7	0.7	0.6	0.97
	Inventory	0.6	0.3	0.1	0.00
	Incident to arrest	9.4	6.0	3.3	0.00

Table C.4—Continued

Year	Legal Basis (sorted roughly from high to low discretion)	Black Drivers (%)	Nonblack Drivers (%)		p-Value
			Matched	Unmatched	
2005		n = 19,375	n = 6,141	n = 25,163	
	Consent	3.8	3.9	2.0	0.70
	Reasonable suspicion of weapon	0.8	0.3	0.1	0.00
	Dog alert	0.0	0.0	0.0	0.01
	Odor (alcohol or drugs)	0.9	0.3	0.2	0.00
	Other probable cause	0.7	0.8	0.4	0.81
	Plain view	0.5	0.5	0.3	0.52
	Inventory	0.6	0.5	0.1	0.36
	Incident to arrest	2.9	2.3	0.9	0.00
2006		n = 20,146	n = 5,365	n = 24,383	
	Consent	3.9	4.9	2.2	0.05
	Reasonable suspicion of weapon	0.7	0.5	0.2	0.12
	Dog alert	0.1	0.0	0.0	0.00
	Odor (alcohol or drugs)	0.6	0.4	0.2	0.32
	Other probable cause	0.7	0.8	0.4	0.30
	Plain view	0.3	0.2	0.1	0.20
	Inventory	0.5	0.6	0.1	0.82
	Incident to arrest	3.5	2.8	1.2	0.02

Table C.4—Continued

Year	Legal Basis (sorted roughly from high to low discretion)	Black Drivers (%)	Nonblack Drivers (%)		p-Value
			Matched	Unmatched	
2007		n = 22,479	n = 4,996	n = 24,220	
	Consent	3.1	4.2	2.0	0.001
	Reasonable suspicion of weapon	0.7	0.2	0.2	0.99
	Dog alert	0.1	0.0	0.0	—
	Odor (alcohol or drugs)	0.7	0.4	0.2	0.03
	Other probable cause	0.7	0.6	0.3	0.95
	Plain view	0.2	0.1	0.1	0.44
	Inventory	0.6	0.6	0.2	0.61
	Incident to arrest	4.0	4.5	1.6	0.27
2008		n = 26,941	n = 4,952	n = 25,149	
	Consent	2.5	4.5	2.0	<0.001
	Reasonable suspicion of weapon	0.8	0.0	0.2	1.0
	Dog alert	0.3	0.1	0.0	0.005
	Odor (alcohol or drugs)	1.5	0.7	0.3	0.001
	Other probable cause	0.8	1.0	0.4	0.41
	Plain view	0.5	0.4	0.2	0.25
	Inventory	0.9	0.7	0.3	0.43
	Incident to arrest	5.7	6.3	2.9	0.17

APPENDIX D

Comments from the Parties on the Report

The following appendix contains comments from the parties on this report. Per the provisions of the evaluation contract, the comments have been printed as received and were not edited; they were formatted only to make them readable in our publication.

Appendix by ACLU to Year 5 RAND Report

Readers are directed to the ACLU Appendix to the Year 4 RAND report for the most comprehensive review by the ACLU of the issues raised by the various RAND studies and the RAND Reports. This Appendix is limited to the Year 5 Report which is a much more limited study.

These RAND studies are not expert reports designed to determine liability for claims of discrimination. Rather, they are neutral studies designed to review a broad range of police activity that may or may not contribute to the perception still held by many that racial bias plays a role in policing in Cincinnati. As stated last year African Americans are interacting against the police after a history of many years of segregation, Jim Crow Laws, and blatant discriminatory practices. There is a harsh legacy of discrimination to overcome.

Every year we see data that shows why African Americans are reluctant to trust the police. This report is no different. But before we address those issues we should acknowledge again the progress that has been made. The latest crime analyst reports demonstrate the continued reduction of overall crime in Cincinnati. That is good. We also note that the City Manager continues to meet with an advisory group that includes the Collaborative parties and stakeholders in order to maintain the broad perspectives on policing that are needed to continue improving relations. That is good. Finally we note that the CPD continues its commitment to problem solving and the use of data to frame its enforcement efforts. Problem solving provides a clear rationale for policing actions and will reduce the harsh racial impact of police actions. Should this be more developed? Yes. But what is happening is good. We encourage these efforts by the CPD and we encourage continued reference to the recommendations set out in the Final Report of the Monitor, December 2008, www.cincinnatimonitor.org

This report looks at three questions (1) Is there a department wide bias in traffic stops? (2) Are there individual CPD officers who stop a disproportionate number of African Americans? (3) Are there racial differences in post- stop outcomes? Even when analyzing these narrow questions we can see the source of continued perceptions of racial bias.

1. **Burden of Policing Disproportionately Impacts African Americans**. RAND accurately notes at p. 50, "although black and similarly situated nonblack drivers have similar stop outcomes, the burden of policing falls disproportionately on black residents." (emphasis added). This has been a constant observation in all five reports. This must be openly and regularly discussed by the CPD with the community so community leaders accept those strategies that are appropriate to the problem and reject those strategies where the impact on peaceful citizens does not support the action. For example, once again we see that "officers more frequently search black drivers than nonblack drivers (13 percent versus 6 percent). While this disparity is largely due to differences in when, where, and why the stops occurred, these differences in experience can shape black drivers' views of CPD officers." That caution must be heeded. Why are there more stops of black drivers? Can the CPD bring down that number? If not can the CPD explain that discrepancy to the community? Is there a way to satisfy the community that "when, where, and

why" stops occur are not in fact pretexts for bias? The CPD has moved away from reliance on some of the strategies that have the heaviest impact on the black community. That has helped improve relations. But that work is obviously not done.

2. **Ten Officers Stop Disproportionate Numbers of African American Motorists**. The data collection and analysis tools adopted during the term of the Collaborative agreement permit these officers to be identified and their policing reviewed. The City must assure the public that a thorough review will be conducted of these ten officers and that discipline will be imposed if they are in fact engaging in biased policing. Further, the ACLU urges the CPD to continue the videotape review of officers doing stops as that can assist leadership in addressing these issues.
3. **False Hits During Discretionary Stops**. Look at the Table 4.2. RAND reports that there is no difference between whites and blacks in the contraband hit rate during stops. But the news to the African American Community on this table is the continued disproportionate use of high discretion stops that result in false hits:

Heed these statements from page 46 – 47 of the Report:

> "Even though we found no racial bias, officers conducted 1,324 high-discretion searches of black drivers in 2008 that recovered no contraband. Such stops, which the motorist likely views as being made for no good reason, disproportionately affect the black community and likely contribute to blacks' perceptions of unfair policing that were identified in last year's report (Ridgeway, Schell, Gifford, et al., 2009). While recovery of contraband from high-discretion searches, such as 33 weapon and 474 drug recoveries, can have a social benefit for the Cincinnati community, there is a societal cost for searches that result in no recovery of contraband."

(emphasis added). The ACLU has noted this issue before (the table shows many years of disparate search numbers) but it does not appear that the CPD has taken any steps to reduce the number of searches of African Americans that result in false hits. These searches are more than double the discretionary searches of white citizens. The related issue in these searches which is not addressed in the Year 5 report is the treatment of African American passengers, another source of tension with the police. The ACLU calls on the City to address this problem in a transparent manner so the community knows that progress will be made.

Cincinnati Police Department's Response to RAND's Year Five Evaluation

The Cincinnati Police Department is pleased again with RAND's reported improvement in the quality of data we have provided to them for this analysis. We continuously strive to improve data collection, quality, and analysis efforts to become more strategically effective. Over the course of RAND's evaluation Department efforts have resulted in a great reduction in records missing vital information; dropping from a 16% missing rate in 2004, to less than .5% in 2008. RAND's evaluation, of our operations has provided transparency of our efforts, an endeavor we hope will continue to build community trust and cooperation.

RAND's analysis continues to show no institutionalized department level racial profiling in officers' decisions to make a traffic stop. Regardless of an officer's ability to identify race, the percentage of black drivers stopped remained constant. While RAND did find ten officers making racially disproportionate stops, it is important to note identification of individual officers is not an indictment of their actions, but an indication for further review. We continue to utilize the analysis tool provided to us by RAND to review each identified officer's actions in the totality of circumstances. We appreciate Dr. Ridgeway's efforts in providing us the ability to identify officers stopping drivers of either race at substantially higher rates than we would find in situationally matched stops made by other officers. Identified officers are reviewed as part of a quarterly risk management assessment conducted at the Command Staff level. Officers' activities are reviewed and compared with activity of the officer's respective peer group. Appropriate intervention or corrective action is taken where necessary as part of ongoing risk management. Additionally, all complaints of discrimination are thoroughly investigated by the CCA (Citizens' Complaint Authority) and by the Police Department, reviewed by the City Manager, and appropriate action taken based on the findings.

In addition to the analysis of who is stopped, RAND's analysis of after stop activity continues to demonstrate when drivers are matched for similar situations (time of day, location, reason for stop, validity of driver's license, etc.) there was no significant difference in the length of the stop or the citation rate and blacks were actually less likely to be subjected to a high discretion search (i.e. consent search). Hit rates, that is, when searched driver's likelihood of having contraband found, were relatively equal whether the driver was black or non-black. We continue our efforts through dialogue with community members in order to strategically focus our efforts on the problem locations and individuals responsible for the majority of crime and disorder in our City.

We continue to see improvements in public perception of our officers and their efforts. We know that agency transparency and prompt response to highly charged incidents are key to maintaining a positive relationship with the community. Anecdotally, officers are reporting more persons are stepping up to provide information about criminal activity, initiate cordial conversation, and to just stop them to say "thanks for your service." We recognize however, that a single incident can reverse much of the gain we have come to realize. Police are entrusted to keep people safe and we do not take that commitment lightly. Our members will endeavor to enhance the reputation of the Cincinnati Police Department.

Although the Collaborative Agreement which created the RAND analysis as a component, has concluded we appreciate the ongoing efforts of the Parties as we continue to forge relationships where they have not previously existed. The City Manager continues his work with the Manager's Advisory Committee comprised of community leaders, representatives of the Parties, and members of the Department. The group addresses ongoing issues including enhanced communication within the community and providing outreach, services and programs to groups with specific needs. We appreciate the continued effort to increase greater participation in problem-solving strategies. Through such efforts, we will connect to people who were previously untapped as resources and educate them in the role they play in the public safety of their communities.

References

Ayres, Ian, "Outcome Tests of Racial Disparities in Police Practices," *Justice Research and Policy*, Vol. 4, No. 1, Fall 2002, pp. 131–142. As of July 28, 2009: http://islandia.law.yale.edu/ayers/jrp.pdf

Benjamini, Yoav, and Yosef Hochberg, "Controlling the False Discovery Rate: A Practical and Powerful Approach to Multiple Testing," *Journal of the Royal Statistical Society*, Series B: *Methodological*, Vol. 57, No. 1, 1995, pp. 289–300. As of July 28, 2009:
http://www.biostat.jhsph.edu/~yonchen/Controlling%20the%20false%20discovery%20rate.pdf

Birotte, André Jr., *Training Evaluation and Management System (TEAMS) II Audit, Phase I (Fiscal Year 2007/2008)*, Los Angeles, Calif.: Office of the Inspector General, Los Angeles Police Department, November 6, 2007. As of July 28, 2009: http://www.lacity.org/oig/Reports/TEAMS2F1Report_11-06-07.pdf

DHHS—*see* U.S. Department of Health and Human Services.

Dominitz, Jeff, "How Do the Laws of Probability Constrain Legislative and Judicial Efforts to Stop Racial Profiling?" *American Law and Economics Review*, Vol. 5, No. 2, 2003, pp. 412–432.

Efron, Bradley, "Large-Scale Simultaneous Hypothesis Testing: The Choice of a Null Hypothesis," *Journal of the American Statistical Association*, Vol. 99, No. 465, March 2004, pp. 96–104.

———, *Correlation and Large-Scale Simultaneous Significance Testing*, Department of Statistics, Stanford University, 2005-21B/235, July 2005.

Efron, Bradley, Brit B. Turnbull, and Balasubramanian Narasimhan, "locfdr Vignette: Complete Help Documentation Including Usage Tips and Simulation Example," *The Comprehensive R Archive Network*, November 1, 2007. As of November 3, 2008:
http://cran.r-project.org/web/packages/locfdr/vignettes/locfdr-example.pdf

Fridell, Lorie A., *By the Numbers: A Guide for Analyzing Race Data from Vehicle Stops*, Washington, D.C.: Police Executive Research Forum, 2004. As of November 26, 2007:
http://www.policeforum.org/library.asp?MENU=229

Gallup, Alec M., and Frank Newport, *The Gallup Poll: Public Opinion 2004*, Lanham, Md.: Rowman and Littlefield, 2006.

GAO—*see* U.S. General Accounting Office.

Greenwald, Howard P., *Final Report: Police Vehicle Stops in Sacramento, California*, Los Angeles, Calif.: University of Southern California, October 31, 2001.

Grogger, Jeffrey, and Greg Ridgeway, "Testing for Racial Profiling in Traffic Stops from Behind a Veil of Darkness," *Journal of the American Statistical Association*, Vol. 101, No. 475, September 2006, pp. 878–887. Reprint, as of December 10, 2008:
http://www.rand.org/pubs/reprints/RP1253/

Hallmark, Shauna L., Kim Mueller, and David Veneziano, *Evaluation of Racial Differences in Seat Belt and Child Restraint Use: A Review of Current Literature*, Ames, Iowa: Center for Transportation Research and Education, Iowa State University, 2004. As of November 26, 2007:
http://www.ctre.iastate.edu/reports/seatbelt.pdf

Hamermesh, Daniel S., *Workdays, Workhours, and Work Schedules: Evidence for the United States and Germany*, Kalamazoo, Mich.: W. E. Upjohn Institute for Employment Research, 1996.

In re Cincinnati Policing, 214 F.R.D. 221, S.D. Ohio, April 7, 2003. As of October 1, 2007:
http://www.cincinnati-oh.gov/police/downloads/police_pdf6369.pdf

Kadane, Joseph B., and Norma Terrin, "Missing Data in the Forensic Context," *Journal of the Royal Statistical Society*, Series A: *Statistics in Society*, Vol. 160, No. 2, 1997, pp. 351–357.

Klinger, David A., "Negotiating Order in Patrol Work: An Ecological Theory of Police Response to Deviance," *Criminology*, Vol. 35, No. 2, May 1997, pp. 277–306.

Lamberth, John, "Measuring the Racial/Ethnic Make Up of Traffic: The How, What and Why," presentation at "Confronting Racial Profiling in the 21st Century: Implications for Racial Justice," Boston, Mass.: Institute on Race and Justice, March 8–9, 2003.

Lange, James E., Kenneth O. Blackman, and Mark B. Johnson, *Speed Violation Survey of the New Jersey Turnpike: Final Report*, Calverton, Md.: Public Services Research Institute, 2002.

Ludwig, Jack, "Americans See Racial Profiling as Widespread," Gallup Poll, 2003. As of July 28, 2009:
http://www.gallup.com/poll/8389/americans-see-racial-profiling-widespread.aspx

Mac Donald, Heather, "The Myth of Racial Profiling," *City Journal*, Spring 2001. As of July 27, 2009:
http://www.city-journal.org/html/11_2_the_myth.html

McCaffrey, Daniel F., Greg Ridgeway, and Andrew R. Morral, "Propensity Score Estimation with Boosted Regression for Evaluating Causal Effects in Observational Studies," *Psychological Methods*, Vol. 9, No. 4, December 2004, pp. 403–425. Reprint, as of July 28, 2009:
http://www.rand.org/pubs/reprints/RP1164/

Ridgeway, Greg, "Assessing the Effect of Race Bias in Post–Traffic Stop Outcomes Using Propensity Scores," *Journal of Quantitative Criminology*, Vol. 22, No. 1, March 2006, pp. 1–29. Reprint, as of December 10, 2008:
http://www.rand.org/pubs/reprints/RP1252/

———, *Analysis of Racial Disparities in the New York Police Department's Stop, Question, and Frisk Practices*, Santa Monica, Calif.: RAND Corporation, TR-534-NYCPF, 2007. As of July 27, 2009:
http://www.rand.org/pubs/technical_reports/TR534/

Ridgeway, Greg, and John M. MacDonald, "Doubly Robust Internal Benchmarking and False Discovery Rates for Detecting Racial Bias in Police Stops," *Journal of the American Statistical Association*, Vol. 104, No. 486, June 2009, pp. 661–668. As of September 18, 2009:
http://www.rand.org/pubs/reprints/RP1394/

Ridgeway, Greg, Terry L. Schell, K. Jack Riley, Susan Turner, and Travis L. Dixon, *Police-Community Relations in Cincinnati: Year Two Evaluation Report*, Santa Monica, Calif.: RAND Corporation, TR-445-CC, 2006. As of November 26, 2007:
http://www.rand.org/pubs/technical_reports/TR445/

Ridgeway, Greg, Terry L. Schell, Brian Gifford, Jessica Saunders, Susan Turner, K. Jack Riley, and Travis L. Dixon, *Police-Community Relations in Cincinnati*, Santa Monica, Calif.: RAND Corporation, MG-853-CC, 2009. As of July 27, 2009:
http://www.rand.org/pubs/monographs/MG853/

Riley, K. Jack, Susan Turner, John MacDonald, Greg Ridgeway, Terry L. Schell, Jeremy M. Wilson, Travis L. Dixon, Terry Fain, Dionne Barnes-Proby, and Brent D. Fulton, *Police-Community Relations in Cincinnati*, Santa Monica, Calif.: RAND Corporation, TR-333-CC, 2005. As of July 27, 2009:
http://www.rand.org/pubs/technical_reports/TR333/

Rostker, Bernard D., Lawrence M. Hanser, William M. Hix, Carl Jensen, Andrew R. Morral, Greg Ridgeway, and Terry L. Schell, *Evaluation of the New York City Police Department Firearm Training and Firearm-Discharge Review Process*, Santa Monica, Calif.: RAND Corporation, MG-717-NYPD, 2008. As of July 27, 2009:
http://www.rand.org/pubs/monographs/MG717/

San Jose (Calif.) Police Department, *Vehicle Stop Demographic Study*, San Jose, Calif., 2002.

Schell, Terry L., Greg Ridgeway, Travis L. Dixon, Susan Turner, and K. Jack Riley, *Police-Community Relations in Cincinnati: Year Three Evaluation Report*, Santa Monica, Calif.: RAND Corporation, TR-535-CC, 2007. As of November 3, 2008:
http://www.rand.org/pubs/technical_reports/TR535/

Sherman, Lawrence W., *Scandal and Reform: Controlling Police Corruption*, Berkeley, Calif.: University of California Press, 1978.

Smith, Michael, and Geoffrey Alpert, "Searching for Direction: Courts, Social Science, and the Adjudication of Racial Profiling Claims," *Justice Quarterly*, Vol. 19, No. 4, December 2002, pp. 673–703.

U.S. Census Bureau, *The American Community Survey*, Washington, D.C., last modified November 1, 2007. As of November 27, 2007:
http://www.census.gov/acs/www/

U.S. Department of Health and Human Services, *Federalwide Assurance (FWA) for the Protection of Human Subjects for Domestic (U.S.) Institutions*, Santa Monica, Calif.: RAND Corporation, FWA00003425, through August 8, 2011.

U.S. Department of Justice, City of Cincinnati (Ohio), and Cincinnati Police Department, memorandum of agreement, April 12, 2002. As of July 28, 2009:
http://www.cincinnati-oh.gov/police/downloads/police_pdf5112.pdf

U.S. General Accounting Office, *Racial Profiling: Limited Data Available on Motorist Stops: Report to the Honorable James E. Clyburn, Chairman, Congressional Black Caucus*, Washington, D.C., GAO/GGD-00-41, March 2000. As of July 27, 2009:
http://purl.access.gpo.gov/GPO/LPS7717

Walker, Samuel, "Searching for the Denominator: Problems with Police Traffic Stop Data and an Early Warning System Solution," *Justice Research and Policy*, Vol. 3, No. 1, Spring 2001, pp. 1525–1701.

———, "The Citizen's Guide to Interpreting Traffic Stop Data: Unraveling the Racial Profiling Controversy," unpublished manuscript, 2002.

———, *Early Intervention Systems for Law Enforcement Agencies: A Planning and Management Guide*, Washington, D.C.: Office of Community Oriented Policing Services, 2003a. As of August 18, 2009:
http://www.cops.usdoj.gov/RIC/ResourceDetail.aspx?RID=85

———, *Internal Benchmarking for Traffic Stop Data: An Early Intervention System Approach*, Omaha, Neb.: Police Professionalism Initiative, University of Nebraska, April 2003b. As of July 28, 2009:
http://www.policeforum.org/upload/internalb%5B1%5D_715866088_12302005131511.pdf

Walker, Samuel, and Leigh Herbst, *The Minneapolis CRA Quality Service Audit: A Two-Year Report, 1998–2000—A Report to the Civilian Review Authority*, Omaha, Neb.: University of Nebraska, Department of Criminal Justice, February 2001.

Zingraff, Matthew T., M. Mason, W. R. Smith, D. Tomaskovic-Devey, P. Warren, H. L. McMurray, and C. R. Fenlon, *Evaluating North Carolina State Highway Patrol Data: Citations, Warnings, and Searches in 1998*, report submitted to North Carolina Department of Crime Control and Public Safety and North Carolina State Highway Patrol, 2000.